LITERATURE MADE EASY

CHARLES DICKENS'S

GREAT
EXPECTATIONS

Written by ROISIN M. BABUTA
WITH TONY BUZAN

BARRON'S

CONTENTS

There are five important things you must know about your brain and memory to revolutionize
the way you study:

◆ how your memory
("recall") works *while* you are learning

◆ how your memory works *after* you have finished learning

◆ how to use Mind Maps – a special technique for helping you with all aspects of your studies

◆ how to increase your reading speed

◆ how to prepare for tests and exams.

Recall during learning
— *THE NEED FOR BREAKS*

When you are studying, your memory can concentrate, understand, and remember well for between 20 and 45 minutes at a time. Then it needs a break. If you continue for longer than this without a break your memory starts to break down. If you study for hours nonstop, you will remember only a small fraction of what you have been trying to learn, and you will have wasted hours of valuable time.

So, ideally, *study for less than an hour*, then take a five- to ten-minute break. During the break listen to music, go for a walk, do some exercise, or just daydream. (Daydreaming is a necessary brain-power booster – geniuses do it regularly.) During the break your brain will be sorting out what it has been learning, and you will go back to your books with the new information safely stored and organized in your memory banks. We recommend breaks at regular intervals as you work through the Literature Guides. Make sure you take them!

Recall after learning

– THE WAVES OF YOUR MEMORY

What do you think begins to happen to your memory right after you have finished learning something? Does it immediately start forgetting? No! Your brain actually *increases* its power and continues remembering. For a short time after your study session, your brain integrates the information, making a more complete picture of everything it has just learned. Only then does the rapid decline in memory begin, and as much as 80 percent of what you have learned can be forgotten in a day.

However, if you catch the top of the wave of your memory, and briefly review (look back over) what you have been studying, the memory is imprinted far more strongly, and stays at the crest of the wave for a much longer time. To maximize your brain's power to remember, take a few minutes at the end of a day and use a Mind Map to review what you have learned. Then review it at the end of a week, again at the end of a month, and finally a week before your test or exam. That way you'll ride your memory wave all the way there – and beyond!

The Mind Map®

– A PICTURE OF THE WAY YOU THINK

Do you like taking notes? More important, do you like having to go back over and learn them before tests or exams? Most students I know certainly do not! And how do you take your notes? Most people take notes on lined paper, using blue or black ink. The result, visually, is boring. And what does *your* brain do when it is bored? It turns off, tunes out, and goes to sleep! Add a dash of color, rhythm, imagination, and the whole note-taking process becomes much more fun, uses more of your brain's abilities, and improves your recall and understanding.

Generally, your mind map is highly personal and need not be understandable to any other person. It mirrors *your* brain. Its purpose is to build up your "memory muscle" by creating images that will help you recall instantly the most important points about characters and plot sequences in a work of fiction you are studying.

You will find Mind Maps throughout this book. Study them, add some color, personalize them, and then try drawing your own. You'll remember them far better. Stick them in your files and on your walls for a quick-and-easy review of the topic.

HOW TO DRAW A MIND MAP

1 First of all, briefly examine the Mind Maps and Mini Mind Maps used in this book. What are the common characteristics? All of them use small pictures or symbols, with words branching out from the illustration.

2 Decide which idea or character in the book you want to illustrate and draw a picture, starting in the middle of the page so that you have plenty of room to branch out. Remember that no one expects a young Rembrandt or Picasso here; artistic ability is not as important as creating an image that you (and you alone) will remember. A round smiling (or sad) face might work as well in your memory as a finished portrait. Use marking pens of different colors to make your Mind Map as vivid and memorable as possible.

3 As your thoughts flow freely, add descriptive words and other ideas that connect to the central image. Print clearly, using one word per line if possible.

4 Further refine your thinking by adding smaller branching lines, containing less important facts and ideas, to connect with the main points.

5 Presto! You have a personal outline of your thoughts and concepts about the characters and the plot of the story. It's not a stodgy formal outline, but a colorful image that will stick in your mind, it is hoped, throughout classroom discussions and final exams.

HOW TO READ A MIND MAP

1 Begin in the center, the focus of your topic.
2 The words/images attached to the center are like chapter headings; read them next.
3 Always read out from the center, in every direction (even on the left-hand side, where you will have to read from right to left, instead of the usual left to right).

USING MIND MAPS

Mind Maps are a versatile tool; use them for taking notes in class or from books, for solving problems, for brainstorming with friends, and for reviewing for tests or exams – their uses are endless. You will find them invaluable for planning essays for coursework and exams. Number your main branches in the order in which you want to use them and off you go – the main headings for your essay are done and all your ideas are logically organized.

Preparing for tests and exams

◆ Review your work systematically. Study hard at the beginning of your course, not the end, and avoid "exam panic!"
◆ Use Mind Maps throughout your course, and build a Master Mind Map for each subject, a giant Mind Map that summarizes everything you know about the subject.
◆ Use memory techniques such as mnemonics (verses or systems for remembering things like dates and events).
◆ Get together with one or two friends to study, compare Mind Maps, and discuss topics.

AND FINALLY...

Have *fun* while you learn – it has been shown that students who make their studies enjoyable understand and remember everything better and get the highest grades. I wish you and your brain every success!

(Tony Buzan)

The guide assumes that you have already read *Great Expectations*, although you could read Background and The Story of *Great Expectations* before that. It is best to use the guide alongside the novel. You could read the Who's Who? and Themes sections without referring to the novel, but you will get more out of these sections if you do refer to it to check the points made, especially when thinking about the questions designed to test your recall and help you to think about the novel.

The different sections

The Commentary section can be used in a number of ways. One way is to read a chapter or part of a chapter in the novel, and then read the commentary for that section. Keep on until you come to a test section, test yourself, then take a break. Or, read the Commentary for a chapter, then read that chapter in the novel, then go back to the Commentary. Find out what works best for you.

Topics for Discussion and Brainstorming gives topics that could well appear on exams or provide the basis for coursework. It would be particularly useful for you to discuss them with friends, or brainstorm them using Mind Map techniques (see p. vi).

How to Get an "A" in English Literature gives valuable advice on what to look for in a text, and what skills you need to develop in order to achieve your personal best.

The Exam Essay is a useful night-before reminder of how to tackle exam questions, and Model Answer and Essay Plan gives an example of an "A"-grade essay and the Mind Map and essay plan used to write it.

The questions

Whenever you come across a question in the guide with a star ✪ in front of it, think about it for a moment. You could even jot down a few words to focus your mind. There is not usually a "right" answer to these questions; it is important for you to develop your own opinions if you want to get an "A." The Test Yourself sections are designed to take you about 10–20 minutes each – which will be time well spent. Take a short break after each one.

KEY TO ICONS

Themes

A **theme** is an idea explored by an author. Whenever a theme is dealt with in the guide, the appropriate icon is used. This means you can find where a theme is mentioned just by leafing through the book. Try it now!

Money

Revenge

Class and snobbery

Pursuit and mystery

Justice

Death and loneliness

Guilt and disillusionment

Childhood

Love and forgiveness

STYLE AND LANGUAGE

This heading and icon are used in the Commentary wherever there is a special section on the author's choice of words and use of literary devices.

Dickens's life

If ever there was a "working-class boy made good," it was
Charles Dickens. Born into a humble background in 1812, he
witnessed his parents constantly struggling against poverty – his
father was imprisoned for debt, and Dickens himself at one stage
(age 11) had to work in a sweatshop in order to supplement the
family income. His childhood was often difficult and lonely,
though probably not as bad as he later claimed.

His family was constantly on the move, sometimes living in
Kent, at other times in parts of London. Kent and London
provide settings for *Great Expectations*; they are also the places
in which Dickens spent most of his adult life, showing us that
however imperfect his childhood may have been, he was
strongly attached to his past.

He had a patchy education, being taught partly at home by his
social-climbing mother and partly at a brutal school for boys. At
the age of 15 he became a junior legal clerk, then at 17 a legal
reporter. After a few years he managed to embark on a career in
journalism, in which he excelled. The success of his first novel,
The Pickwick Papers, in 1836, when he was 24, enabled him to
become a full-time novelist.

By the time he died at the age of 57, from a combination of
overwork, kidney disease, and heart failure, he had produced
one of the most important bodies of work in English literature.
He enjoyed wealth, fame, and popularity, yet he was a restless
genius, always searching, never satisfied, always hoping for
something better around the next corner.

Dickens's life recreated in fiction

Two of Dickens's most autobiographical novels are *David
Copperfield* and *Great Expectations*. In both of these, he
recreates the helpless fears and strange emotions of children

1

trapped in an unhappy childhood. Dickens felt strongly that his own parents never gave him the warm security essential to a happy, comfortable childhood. Most literary critics have found *Great Expectations* the more artistic treatment of his childhood experiences.

Dickens's audience

Dickens's readership was drawn from a far wider base than that of previous novelists. The reasons for this can be summed up as follows: **education**, **cheap magazines**, and **railroads**.

The expansion of **education** for all throughout the nineteenth century meant that more people were able to read and write. Dickens's novels were read by members of all social classes, although their greatest appeal was to intelligent working-class and lower middle-class readers.

Dickens wrote for serial publication in popular **magazines**. This meant that all his novels appeared in parts, like weekly or monthly episodes of a soap opera, so that people looked forward to buying their copy to keep up with his latest story. Of course, they also passed the magazines around, as you would do now, so that eventually, just about everyone read them.

Finally, during the nineteenth century there was a rapid expansion of the **railroad** network throughout England. People wanted something to read when they traveled, and these magazines filled the need perfectly. Lending libraries, too, began their existence in railroad stations, giving an enormous boost to the sales of popular novels.

Victorian society

THE CLASS SYSTEM

As Dickens's career prospered, the social fabric of England was changing. Increasing educational opportunities made economic prosperity possible for many more people than before. However, making money through business did not automatically make someone "higher class." Each class had its own manners and customs, even ways of dressing, which could not easily be learned. The emerging middle class and the aspiring working class viewed each other with suspicion, and both in turn were generally despised by the upper class.

Dickens himself was the victim of snobbery and contempt throughout his life. He understood what it was like to belong to one class financially and another by birth. He puts all this understanding – and all the suffering it caused him – into *Great Expectations*.

EDUCATION AND PUBLIC HEALTH

Pip, the central character of *Great Expectations*, suffers from the narrowness of his educational opportunities. Dickens set the novel in a time before the expansion of education in order to demonstrate just how destructive the old educational system was. By the time this novel was written, primary education was available to all but the social lower class, and it was widely accepted that no one should be condemned to a life of illiteracy.

Dickens's age was also one of great public health reform. Education and sanitation were seen as the twin pillars of decency. Dickens himself worked tirelessly publicizing the Metropolitan Sanitary Association and constantly highlighting problems of public health in his novels. In *Great Expectations*, the filth and decay of London is presented as a moral problem; Dickens is as interested in demonstrating the cold and selfish mentality behind such conditions as he is in showing the conditions themselves.

PRISONS AND THE LEGAL SYSTEM

Another target for reformers throughout the nineteenth century was the legal system. Transportation of convicts and imprisonment for debt were both abolished in the 1860s. Dickens's own early experiences with the law gave him a distrust and contempt for the whole system that he never really lost. We have only to look at the character of Jaggers to realize how deep Dickens's feelings went. Justice and "the Law" were often incompatible, in life and in art, and he never lets us forget this.

now that you have some background, take a break before focusing on the plot

connections between events

1 Pip meets a convict on the marshes and tries to help him

2 Pip meets Miss Havisham. Falls in love with her adopted daughter, Estella

3 Pip has a mysterious benefactor who wants to make him a gentleman

4 Pip comes to London. Begins to be embarrassed by his background and to reject Joe

5 Pip falls even more deeply in love with Estella

6 Pip becomes a snob and gets into debt. Returns to forge only for Mrs. Joe's funeral

7 Magwitch returns, reveals himself as Pip's benefactor, and explains his connection to Compeyson and Miss Havisham

8 Miss Havisham regrets her past actions. Pip rescues her from a fire and gets badly burned

9 Orlick tries to murder Pip, but Pip is rescued by Herbert

10 Compeyson catches up with Magwitch, but dies in the struggle

11 Pip stays with the dying Magwitch, and tells him that his daughter is still alive

12 Pip falls ill, and wakes up to see Joe. Joe looks after him until he is better

13 Pip returns to forge, but finds out that it is no longer his home

14 Pip meets Estella in the ruins of Satis House

Pip, an orphan, lives with his sister whom he calls "Mrs. Joe," and his brother-in-law, Joe Gargery, a **blacksmith**, in Kent. One day he meets a **convict** out on the marshes and helps him. The convict is recaptured after a fight with another escaped convict, his enemy, **Compeyson**. Shortly afterward, Pip is asked by Uncle **Pumblechook**, a local shopkeeper, to visit Miss **Havisham** at **Satis House**. Time has stopped for her ever since she was **deserted** on her wedding day. Pip falls hopelessly in love with **Estella**, Miss Havisham's adopted daughter. On one occasion, he has a fight with a young man on the grounds of the house. Pip quickly becomes a **snob**, rejecting Joe and his working-class origins. However, he is apprenticed to Joe. Mrs. Joe is disabled by a **hammer attack** from Joe's assistant, **Orlick**.

Pip is delighted when he receives a fortune from a mysterious **benefactor**. Jaggers, the **lawyer**, informs Pip, allowing him to believe that the benefactor is Miss Havisham. Pip goes to live in **London**.

Jaggers, now Pip's **guardian**, sets Pip up with a roommate, **Herbert** Pocket, who turns out to be the boy Pip fought at Satis House. Pip studies with Herbert's father, **Matthew**, to learn to be a "**gentleman**," along with Bentley **Drummle** and **Startop**. Estella, now very beautiful, is successfully pursued by Drummle. While Pip becomes friends with Jaggers's clerk, **Wemmick**, he never gets to know Jaggers and is puzzled by Jaggers's housekeeper, **Molly**. Pip and Herbert fall heavily into **debt**.

Joe visits Pip once in London, but Pip returns to the **forge** only when Mrs. Joe **dies**, although he has made visits to Satis House. Pip always assumes that his money comes from Miss Havisham. This belief is shattered one night when "Pip's convict," **Abel Magwitch**, returns to England after serving a sentence of transportation in **Australia**. When Pip realizes that Magwitch is his real **benefactor**, he sees that his dreams about Estella and Miss Havisham were an **illusion**.

Pip confides in **Herbert**. It soon becomes clear that the other convict, **Compeyson**, who originally tricked Magwitch and received a much **shorter** sentence, is also in London, pursuing Magwitch. As Magwitch faces the **death penalty** by returning to England if caught by the police, Pip and Herbert feel responsible for him. **Compeyson** turns out to be the man who abandoned Miss Havisham and who had been conspiring with her half-brother **Arthur** to swindle her. **Molly**, Jaggers's housekeeper, turns out to be Estella's mother. Many years before, Molly had been married to Magwitch, and Jaggers had gotten her off a **murder** charge. Jaggers gave the three-year-old child of Molly and Magwitch (thought by Magwitch to have been killed) to Miss Havisham to adopt.

Wemmick, Pip, and Herbert have a plan to get Magwitch (now called **Provis**) abroad and out of danger. Meanwhile, Miss Havisham repents her cruelty and asks Pip's **forgiveness**. Estella is now married to **Drummle**. Pip tries to rescue Miss Havisham from a fire, although she dies later. Pip is summoned to the **limekiln** near his own village by an anonymous letter, where he meets **Orlick**, who has been following him in London. Orlick tries to kill him, but Pip is saved by Herbert and **Startop**.

They fail to save **Magwitch**, as they are overtaken in their escape down the Thames by the **river police** with Compeyson on board (he, too, has been **following** Pip). Compeyson and Magwitch struggle again, and this time Compeyson is drowned and Magwitch fatally wounded. He dies in **prison** with Pip at his side. When Magwitch is on his death bed, Pip tells him that his **daughter** is alive, and that he and the **daughter** are in love.

Herbert goes to **Egypt** after Pip has secretly used some of his own money and some of Miss Havisham's to set him up in business. Pip is left alone. He becomes very ill with a **fever**, but is rescued and looked after by **Joe**, who also pays off his debts. Repenting his **snobbery**, he returns to Kent, hoping to marry Biddy, his childhood friend, but finds she has married Joe. He goes **abroad**, returning 11 years later. He meets Estella (Drummle is now dead) in the **ruins** of Satis House, and there is a hint that they will be united.

How much can you remember?

Try to fill in the words missing from this summary without looking at the original. Feel free to use your own words if they have the same meaning.

Pip, an orphan, lives with his sister, Mrs. Joe, and his brother-in-law, Joe, a _____, in Kent. One day he meets a _____ out on the marshes and helps him. The convict is recaptured after a fight with another escaped convict, his enemy, _____. Shortly afterward, Pip is asked by Uncle _____, a local shopkeeper, to visit Miss _____ at _____ _____. Time has stopped for her ever since she was _____ on her wedding day. Pip falls hopelessly in love with _____, Miss Havisham's adopted daughter. On one occasion, he has a fight with a young man on the grounds of the house. Pip quickly becomes a _____, rejecting Joe and his working-class origins. However, he is apprenticed to Joe. Mrs. Joe is disabled by a _____ _____ from Joe's assistant, _____.

Pip is delighted when he receives a fortune from a mysterious _____. Jaggers, the _____, informs Pip and lets him believe that the benefactor is Miss Havisham. Pip goes to live in _____.

Jaggers, now Pip's _____, sets Pip up with a roommate, _____ Pocket, who turns out to be the boy Pip fought at Satis House. Pip studies with Herbert's father, Matthew, to learn to be a "_____," along with Bentley _____ and _____. Estella, now very beautiful, is successfully pursued by Drummle. While Pip becomes friends with Jaggers's clerk, _____, he never gets to know Jaggers and is puzzled by Jaggers's housekeeper, _____. Pip and Herbert fall heavily into _____.

Joe visits Pip once in London, but Pip returns to the _____ only when Mrs. Joe _____ , although he has made visits to Satis House. Pip always assumes that his money comes from Miss Havisham. This belief is shattered one night when "Pip's convict," _____ _____, returns to England after serving a sentence of transportation in _____. When Pip realizes that Magwitch is his real _____, he sees that his dreams about Estella and Miss Havisham were an _____.

Pip confides in _____. It soon becomes clear that the other convict, _____, who originally tricked Magwitch and received a much _____ sentence, is also in London, pursuing Magwitch. As Magwitch faces the _____ _____ by returning to England if caught by the police, Pip and Herbert feel responsible for him. _____ turns out to be the man who abandoned Miss Havisham and who had been conspiring with her half-brother, _____, to swindle her. _____, Jaggers's housekeeper, turns out to be Estella's mother. Many years before, Molly had been married to Magwitch, and Jaggers had gotten her off a _____ charge. Jaggers gave the three-year-old child of Molly and Magwitch (thought by Magwitch to have been killed) to Miss Havisham to adopt.

Wemmick, Pip, and Herbert have a plan to get Magwitch (now called _____) abroad and out of danger. Meanwhile, Miss Havisham repents her cruelty and asks Pip's _____. Estella is now married to _____. Pip tries to rescue Miss Havisham from a fire, although she dies later. Pip is summoned to the _____ near his own village by an anonymous letter, where he meets _____, who has been following him in London. Orlick tries to kill him, but Pip is saved by Herbert and _____.

They fail to save _____, as they are overtaken in their escape down the Thames by the _____ _____ with Compeyson on board (he, too, has been _____ Pip). Compeyson and Magwitch struggle again, and this time Compeyson is drowned and Magwitch fatally wounded. He dies in _____ with Pip at his side. When Magwitch is on his death bed, Pip tells him that his _____ is alive, and that he and the _____ are in love.

Herbert goes to _____ after Pip has secretly used some of his own money and some of Miss Havisham's to set him up in business. Pip is left alone. He becomes very ill with a _____, but is rescued and looked after by Joe, who also pays off his debts. Repenting his _____, he returns to Kent, hoping to marry Biddy, his childhood friend, but finds she has married Joe. He goes _____, returning 11 years later. He meets Estella (Drummle is now dead) in the _____ of Satis House, and there is a hint that they will be united.

when you've seen how well you did, take a break before finding out who's who

WHO'S WHO?

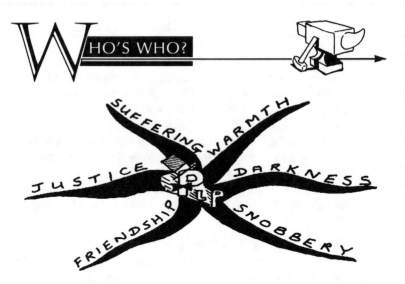

The Mini Mind Map above summarizes the characters in *Great Expectations*. Test yourself by looking at the full Mind Map on p. 19 and then copying the Mini Mind Map and trying to add to it from memory.

P*ip*

His real name is Philip Pirrip, an orphan living with his much older sister, "Mrs. Joe," and her husband, Joe Gargery, at a blacksmith's forge in an unnamed village in Kent. He is the narrator of the story. At the beginning of the novel he is seven years old, and we follow his story until he is 23. At first, he is an innocent boy growing up in a poor background, but then contact with Miss Havisham and Estella turns him into a snob. After he is given a mysterious income, he leaves Kent, lives in London, and becomes lonely and corrupt. He almost loses our sympathy, but still has traces of goodness and generosity that keep us from despising him. Through his own cruelty to Joe and his experiences with the convict, he learns the true meaning of love and friendship. Humbled by the kindness of both these men, he becomes more unselfish, loses his immature snobbery, and is finally reunited with Estella.

Abel Magwitch

Pip's convict or "Provis." First seen on the marshes after escaping from the convict ships, *the hulks*, he gets Pip to help him. He is recaptured after fighting with his enemy, Compeyson, and transported for his crimes to Australia. In the course of the novel we discover that Magwitch, Compeyson, and Miss Havisham's half-brother, Arthur, swindled Miss Havisham out of her money. Compeyson also jilted her on her wedding day. Magwitch had been married to a woman who was tried for murder and acquitted, with Jaggers's help. They had a little girl (Estella) whom Jaggers decided to give to Miss Havisham to look after. As a way of thanking Pip for his help, and because Pip reminds him of his own child, Magwitch decides to make Pip a "gentleman." He works hard in Australia, becomes wealthy, and sends the money back to Pip. When Pip is 23, Magwitch returns to England, risking death to reveal himself to his "boy." Pip tries to help him flee the country, but they are tracked down by the police with Compeyson's help. Magwitch is fatally injured after struggling in the river with Compeyson, and dies in prison with Pip at his side.

Joe Gargery

The novel's gentle giant, the blacksmith at the forge in Kent, and husband of Pip's sister. He loves Pip like his own son and often protects him from Mrs. Joe's anger. His favorite phrases to Pip are *wot larks* and *ever the best of friends*. He is illiterate, and the young Pip mistakenly thinks he is stupid. As Pip's snobbery grows, he comes to look down on Joe and finds him embarrassing and uneducated. He stops visiting the forge, returning only for Mrs. Joe's funeral, and Joe moves out of the story. Joe returns to look after Pip when he is ill, being just as generous and good as before. At the end of the novel, Joe marries Biddy and they have their own family, including a *little Pip*. Joe is the novel's moral center, a figure of complete kindness and simplicity, referred to by Pip as *this gentle Christian man*.

Miss Havisham

Pip calls her *the strangest lady I have ever seen.* She is an old woman living in Satis House, a big old house near Pip's village, with Estella, her adopted daughter. She has not left the house since being jilted on her wedding day, and she still wears her faded wedding dress. The wedding cake is still decaying on the table, and the house is almost in ruins. We learn that Miss Havisham's mother died when she was a baby and that her father, a gentleman brewer, left her a lot of money when he died. Her lover, Compeyson, conspired with her half-brother Arthur, and jilted her. Since then, she has sworn revenge on men and uses Estella to exact this revenge. Pip goes to play at her house and falls in love with Estella. He assumes that Miss Havisham is his benefactor – she lets him think so – and she encourages him to love Estella. The old woman is later horrified by his suffering and regrets her actions. She almost dies in a fire, but Pip rescues her. She dies soon afterward, asking Pip to forgive her.

Estella Havisham

Cold, hard, and unfeeling, like the stars for which she is named, Estella's heartless presence dominates the novel. She is the daughter of Abel Magwitch and Molly, Mr. Jaggers's housekeeper, rescued by Jaggers after her mother was acquitted of murder and her father transported. Miss Havisham's use of her as a weapon in a war against all men has made her cynical and ruthless. She torments Pip when they are younger, calling him a *common boy,* and he remains obsessed with her throughout his life. They stay friends while Estella lives in London. She makes a loveless but socially correct marriage to Bentley Drummle, who mistreats her. After his death she and Pip are apparently reunited. Estella, like Pip, has learned through her mistakes and is more humble and less arrogant at the end of the novel.

Herbert Pocket

Son of Matthew Pocket, one of Miss Havisham's relatives. Herbert first appears, unnamed (the *pale young gentleman*) in the gardens of Satis House on one of Pip's first visits (Chapter

11). He challenges Pip to a fight and Pip beats him. Herbert is very easygoing about the whole thing. We don't see him again until the end of Chapter 21, when he reappears at Pip's boarding house in London. He is kind, generous, and not very good with money. He is a very good friend to Pip ("Handel," as he calls him). They get drunk together, and get into debt together. Herbert advises Pip about how to improve his manners, listens to his complaints about Estella, and helps him with Magwitch. He also inspires Pip's one real gesture of financial generosity. Pip sets Herbert up in business with Clarriker. Herbert marries Clara Barley and goes on to make a success of his business. He is an essential contrast to Pip (who is selfish and snobbish) and an important symbol of friendship and unselfishness.

Mr. Jaggers

Positioned at the novel's center, Jaggers is the keeper of the characters' secrets, and a symbol of the ambiguity of justice.

Like Herbert, Jaggers enters the novel unnamed, in Chapter 11. Little Pip's first impressions are of someone who has *sharp and suspicious* eyes and a large watch chain, and who smells of soap. He is Miss Havisham's and Magwitch's lawyer and Pip's guardian. In Chapter 18, he reenters dramatically, revealing details of Pip's *great expectations* (he is the first to use the ironic phrase – **ironic**, because things do not turn out as well for Pip as the phrase suggests), and summoning him to London. Joe has a negative impression of Jaggers. He is surrounded by an aura of great power and control, and he always makes Pip feel guilty.

Jaggers is also a respected defense and prosecution lawyer; Chapter 20 focuses on the corrupt and capitalistic atmosphere in which he works and shows his connection with the seamier side of life. He acquits and protects Molly, Magwitch's wife (probably a murderess), and uncharacteristically saves Estella by giving her to Miss Havisham.

We, like Pip, are angry with him because of his deliberate withholding of information from Pip. His power over Molly suggests a dark and sinister side to his character, as does his

attraction to "The Spider" (Drummle). In the end, he is the only major character in the novel who seems to show no remorse whatever for his part in Pip's tragedy. It is no coincidence that Jaggers's area of London is called "Little Britain," a small but accurate reflection of Great Britain itself.

John Wemmick

Jaggers's clerk (assistant), Wemmick is one of many characters in the novel whom Pip initially misjudges. To begin with, Pip sees him as *a dry man . . . with a square wooden face,* but soon learns that this is just a "Little Britain" facade, a way of protecting his private life. When he is in the City of London, he is efficient, unemotional, and highly secretive; in Walworth, where he lives with his "Aged P," he is gentle, resourceful, and helpful. The contrast between the two Wemmicks is so marked that on one occasion Pip feels *as if there were twin Wemmicks and this was the wrong one.* Wemmick is a loyal and tireless friend to Pip. He helps him set Herbert up in business; he warns him about Compeyson (*Don't go home*); he is part of the plan to get Magwitch abroad; and he helps Pip unravel all the mysteries surrounding Estella, Miss Havisham, and the convict.

Wemmick makes us aware of the deep flaws in a society that requires us to suppress our kindness and morality in order to get ahead. In order to do his job properly, Wemmick literally has to "put away" his normal, healthy, human feelings. When he crosses the drawbridge to his castle, he is retreating back to these values, away from the corruption of Jaggers and the city.

Minor Characters

Mrs. Joe is Pip's sister, 20 years older than he. She is not a complex, fully rounded character, but a caricature, not meant to seem real. Her tall, bony frame seems more masculine than motherly, and her erratic behavior sets the tone for the whole novel. She is a cruel, violent woman, as sharp and unsympathetic as the pins and needles stuck into the front of her apron. Her treatment of Pip shows contempt and a lack of understanding for children. Without the verbal humor (*I often served as a connubial missile*), her behavior would be intolerable for the reader. As it is, she provides us with some moments of rich comedy. She is also at the center of one of the novel's most vicious episodes, when Orlick, in a gesture of revenge for her harsh words, disables her with a blow from his hammer. After this climactic episode she fades from view until Biddy describes her death in Chapter 35. It is a very moving speech, and we are surprised by Mrs. Joe's remorse and the peacefulness of her death. Like many other characters in the novel, she is not exactly what she seems.

Biddy, like Mrs. Joe, is not a particularly realistic character. She is Pip's friend from childhood. Largely self-educated, she becomes the village schoolmistress. In a conventional fairy-tale ending, she marries Joe and they have a lot of children. As far as Dickens's readers were concerned, this was the reward for her virtue and morality throughout the novel.

Biddy has a vital function in the novel. She gently reminds Pip of how wrong he is to patronize, and later to neglect, Joe. This happens on a number of occasions, notably in Chapter 19 and again in Chapter 35. These dialogues are memorable because they contrast so sharply with all Pip's conversations with Estella. Biddy's moral superiority is obvious to Pip, and to us, and yet we can understand Pip's infatuation with Estella. Biddy represents the warmth, generosity, honesty, and morality of the "respectable working class." In many ways, Pip does not really deserve her, which is why we're not disappointed when his plan to marry her fails.

Of all the characters in the novel, **Orlick** is the most strange and surprising. His origins are mysterious, and his status at the forge is always in some doubt. The violence in the novel often centers on Orlick; in an act of revenge and hatred, he paralyzes Mrs. Joe and he does his best to kill Pip. He also pursues Pip through London, becoming a kind of shadow, perhaps even Pip's own dark side. His hatred of Pip seems out of all proportion to the events of the novel, but it is still entirely convincing.

Finally, Orlick's violence toward Pip completes the hellish physical torture Pip undergoes before his change of heart in the last part of the novel. In this respect he is an essential component of Pip's growth into a more humble and more humane adult.

In one sense, **Compeyson** is the most minor of all the minor characters as his appearances in the novel are so brief; yet he is possibly the most important character in the entire plot. The man who jilted Miss Havisham and who betrayed Magwitch, he links the two characters with the strongest influence on Pip. He is described as a *gentleman* (the very thing Pip wants to become) and yet Dickens gives him no redeeming features whatever. Heartless, manipulative, and cynical, his life is devoted entirely to his own gains, with no sign of humanity or remorse. We see him locked in violent conflict with Magwitch (Chapter 5 and again, fatally, in Chapter 54). The rest of the time, he is a menacing, shadowy presence, haunting the novel and pursuing Pip silently through the London streets. He is in every sense a "ghost from the past," and it is only after his death that either Pip or Magwitch is able to be at peace.

Bentley Drummle is a student at Matthew Pocket's, a friend of Jaggers. Another "gentleman," Estella's future husband is presented through Pip's angry and jealous eyes as being *sulky, disagreeable*, arrogant, and callous. His pursuit of Estella is purely acquisitive and after their marriage he becomes violent to her and is finally killed in a riding accident.

Startop, the other student, initially makes little impression, but proves to be loyal and reliable. He unselfishly agrees to help Pip and Herbert in their plans for Magwitch. He helps Herbert to save Pip at the limekiln and then shares the rowing with Herbert during the escape. He shows another side of "gentlemanliness," not destructive, but quiet and modest.

The Pockets are a chaotic family. Matthew Pocket advised Miss Havisham many years before the opening of the novel not to become involved with Compeyson. As a result of this, Miss Havisham turns against Matthew. She finally forgives him on Pip's advice and leaves him money in her will. He is a kind but not very strict father and makes his money by teaching young men to be gentlemen. His wife is from an old aristocratic family and cannot run the house efficiently.

Uncle Pumblechook is Joe's friend. He runs a corn and seed shop in the village. He is a terrible (comic) snob and has the habit of only ever communicating with Pip by giving him arithmetic problems to do. It is through him that Pip originally comes into contact with Miss Havisham. He then tries to prove that he was the original source of Pip's *great expectations* and that Pip owes everything to him. Pip dislikes him intensely.

Wopsle is a very bad amateur actor. The occasional trips to his performances give the novel its finest comic scenes. He provides light relief and gives Pip the crucial information that Compeyson is following him in London.

Molly was married to Magwitch many years before the story opens. They had a baby daughter. She is acquitted of the murder of another woman and then goes to work for Jaggers, who had represented her, as his housekeeper. Jaggers "saves" Molly's three-year-old daughter, whom Magwitch assumes is dead, and gives her to Miss Havisham to adopt. She is around 40 years old when Pip sees her, and she reminds him of one of the witches in *Macbeth*.

Arthur Havisham was Miss Havisham's half-brother. He teamed up with Compeyson and helped to swindle Miss Havisham out of her money. However, he regretted his callous act and died hallucinating about a *woman in white*.

Clara Barley is Herbert Pocket's fiancée. She looks after her father and helps Pip by hiding Magwitch at her lodgings in Mill Pond Bank. She marries Herbert. **Old Barley** is her eccentric, drunken father. **Mrs. Whimple** is the Barleys' landlady.

Trabb is the tailor in Pip's village. He makes Pip new clothes when he comes into money. He also organizes Mrs. Joe's funeral. **Trabb's boy** is Trabb's assistant, a comic figure. He always laughs at Pip behind his back, but helps to save Pip's life at the limekiln.

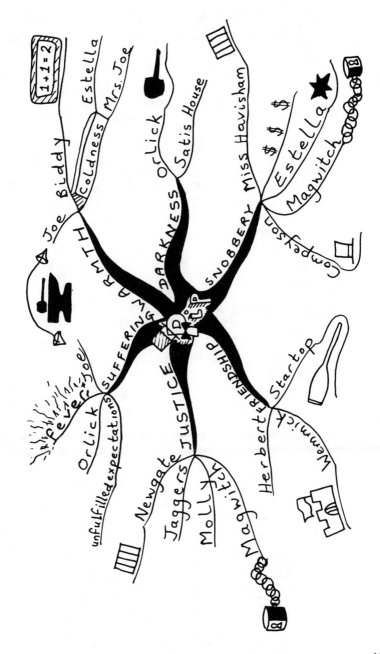

THEMES

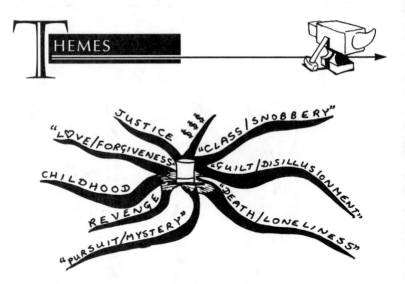

A theme is an idea developed or explored throughout a work. The Mini Mind Map above shows the main themes of *Great Expectations*. Test yourself by copying the Mini Mind Map, adding to it, and then comparing your results with the version on p. 19.

Money

Victorian society was built on a belief in capitalism, but in this novel money is seen as a corrupting force. Pip's money inspires him to abandon Joe, the forge, and his real moral values, and to live a degraded life in London. It is partly a materialistic desire for something "valuable," which makes him obsessed with Estella. Greed for money drove Magwitch and Compeyson into their plot against Miss Havisham. Magwitch believes that his money will free Pip from his poverty, when, in fact, it imprisons him still further and is finally confiscated. Money drives Jaggers, while his clerk Wemmick's passion for *portable property* reveals an unpleasant side to an essentially good character. The characters in the novel who display the greatest warmth, love, and unselfishness are those who are unconcerned with wealth (Joe, Biddy) or incapable of making money without benevolent assistance (Herbert Pocket).

Class and snobbery

Closely linked to material wealth is the concept of class, and the snobbery that goes with it. Dickens ruthlessly exposes Pip's snobbish desire to be a gentleman and to live in the same exalted circle as Estella and Miss Havisham. Estella turns out to be the daughter of a convict and a murderess, so her "class" is in fact an illusion. The most socially elevated characters in the novel are also some of the most repulsive: Miss Havisham (deranged), Bentley Drummle (violent and destructive), and Mrs. Pocket (lazy and incompetent). Compeyson's "gentlemanliness" is what gets him off lightly, while Magwitch has to pay the full price for his crimes. The characters who cluster round Miss Havisham are equally negative. Again, the characters who form the moral center of the novel, Joe and Biddy, are from the respectable working class. Pip returns to their values once he has acknowledged the hollowness and corruption of his dreams. By this time he is a gentleman in the true, deeper sense of the word.

Justice

Dickens exposes the legal system as being entirely corrupt. Jaggers's rejection of any responsibility for Pip's mistakes and his lack of moral perspective about his clients make him a dark and sinister character. Newgate prison seems to radiate decay and to poison the streets around it. The novel is full of little prisons: Satis House, Wemmick's Castle, Jaggers's office, Magwitch's final home with Clara Barley. Miss Havisham is unjustly treated, Magwitch is unjustly punished, Pip treats Joe and Biddy with no respect for justice. Orlick seizes his own chance for justice in his revenge on Pip. The justice that finally hunts Magwitch down is harsh and unforgiving.

Despite all of this, there is a natural justice at work: Joe and Biddy deserve each other; Herbert wins good-natured Clara Barley and makes the best of Pip's money; Pip is rewarded with Estella only after intense suffering; Miss Havisham dies in a fire symbolic of her own vengeful nature; Estella pays for her coldness in an unhappy marriage to Bentley Drummle;

Magwitch's hard work and unselfishness are finally rewarded by the sight of his "gentleman."

Guilt and disillusionment

Guilt drives the narrative. It gives the novel its melancholy tone and its extraordinary clarity. Pip's initial childish guilt stems from being told by adults that he should never have been born and from the help he secretly gives to the convict. Pip is ashamed of Joe, but constantly guilty about his own attitudes when Joe is in London. He is guilty about his debts. Just being with Jaggers makes him feel guilty. This heavy burden is only lightened by suffering; by the end of the novel, his conscience is finally clear. He is subdued and humbled, but no longer haunted by remorse.

Love and forgiveness

The regretful tone of the novel is balanced by the constant presence of selfless love, personified by Joe. Joe's simplicity demonstrates the power of love to overcome rejection and absence. After Pip has been ill, Joe's generosity to him is as unquestioning and unreserved as when Pip was a small child. Through him, and through Magwitch's selfless, though misguided, protection, Pip perceives the coldness at the heart of his ambitions. He is constantly protected by loving friends – Herbert, Wemmick, Biddy – but only realizes their true value at the end of the novel.

He has been misled by the powerful but destructive force of his infatuation with Estella. Thwarted love perverts Miss Havisham, who, in turn, twists Estella, whose influence nearly destroys Pip. Pip knows this, but forgives Miss Havisham and Estella for their part in his tragedy. Joe and Biddy forgive him for his arrogance. Pip is so humbled by his experiences that he is able to forgive the convict who shapes his life. This strongly Christian theme drives the final part of the novel, when Pip himself is at last able to emerge from his guilt and regret into an atmosphere of warmth and companionship.

Revenge

The revenge theme is what gives the novel its "mystery thriller" structure. Magwitch is grimly determined to avenge himself on the treacherous, exploitative Compeyson. Miss Havisham's education of Estella is a revenge against all men. Orlick, in the most sensational of all the variations on the theme, takes violent revenge on Mrs. Joe for insulting him and tries to do the same to Pip just for being who he is. In the end, the legal system takes revenge on Magwitch rather than punishing him fairly.

This theme lends excitement and narrative drive to the novel, inspiring the reader to follow the plot through to its conclusion.

Pursuit and mystery

The motif of pursuit fits the "sensational" framework of the novel and is closely linked with the revenge theme. Magwitch pursues Compeyson; both are pursued by the Law across the marshes, and finally, Magwitch is overtaken by Justice. Orlick pursues Pip and nearly kills him. Pip pursues a misguided idea of gentlemanliness. A notable feature of the last stage of the novel is Pip's conviction that he is constantly being watched.

The idea of the chase is central to some of the novel's great set-piece chapters: Chapter 5, when Magwitch is hunted across the marshes, and Chapter 54, when they try to smuggle him out of the country.

Adding to the thriller element in the novel is its web of secrets and mystery. The plot hinges on the secret source of Pip's money, and the revelation of Magwitch as his benefactor is one of the novel's most effective climaxes. The slow process of unraveling the different mysteries linking the characters holds the novel together and urges the reader on.

Jaggers is at the center of all the novel's secrets and his power comes from not disclosing any of his knowledge. The secrecy that he sees as a necessary part of his job is, in fact, highly destructive. He does nothing to prevent Pip's tragedy.

Death and loneliness

Death punctuates the novel regularly and significantly. Pip himself is an orphan and, therefore, particularly lonely and vulnerable; we first see him among the graves of his family. Mrs. Joe's death gives us an unexpected moment of great beauty and reminds Pip of the shortness of life. Miss Havisham's death demonstrates the self-destructive power of revenge. Magwitch's death movingly highlights Pip's transformation into a generous and forgiving adult. The violent death of Compeyson satisfies our desire for justice, as does the death of Bentley Drummle.

All the characters in the novel battle against loneliness and try to give their lives meaning, most of all Pip himself. The first-person narrative casts a melancholy tone over the whole novel, making us constantly aware of how fragile happiness really is and how alone in the world we all are.

Childhood

Dickens always campaigned passionately for the rights of children, particularly those without a loving, stable family background. In *Great Expectations* he writes movingly and sometimes humorously of the fears and humiliations of childhood.

Pip is an orphan whose early childhood is dominated by the loneliness and desolation of the marshes, a monotony relieved by the warmth of the forge fire. He lives under constant threat from the adult world—physically oppressed by Mrs. Joe, looked upon as a burden by her friends.

He is acutely sensitive to humiliation. Estella makes him feel coarse and common; yet he wants only to be part of her world. Satis House is always seen from a child's viewpoint: gothic, surreal, and very much larger than life. The older Pip constantly points out the significance of these early influences on his later development.

Other children in the novel are equally disadvantaged. Estella is apparently an orphan, the child of a murderess and a convict. The Pocket children grow up in a state of neglect. Magwitch spent his childhood wandering the streets scratching for a living. Dickens found his most intense inspiration for this novel in his own feelings of loss at the premature ending of his own childhood, and the influence of his own melancholy viewpoint is present throughout.

now you understand the main themes. Take a break before using the Mind Map on p. 26 to check your recall

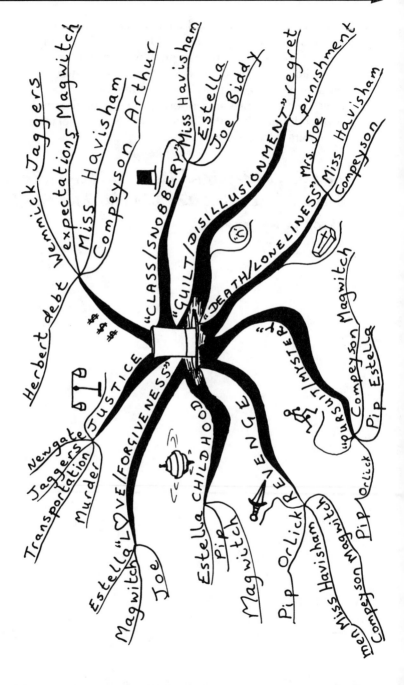

L ANGUAGE, STYLE, AND STRUCTURE

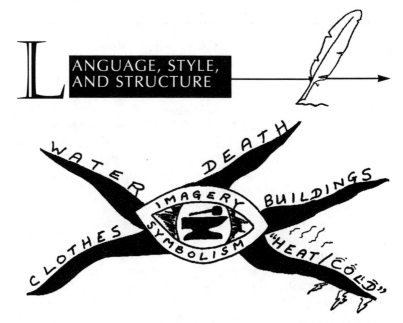

The main features of language, style, and structure in *Great Expectations* are shown in the Mini Mind Map above. Copy it and add to it as you go along. Test yourself on imagery using the Mind Map on p. 32.

Structure

The main structure of the novel derives from the use of the first-person retrospective narrative. (The story is told by Pip, looking back at his past.) Pip's development falls into three sections, each charting a separate stage in his expectations. It is also structured in terms of place: Kent (country) / London (city), and moves constantly from warmth (friendship, love, forgiveness) to cold (Estella, the marshes, revenge, pursuit). Dickens also uses water, the river, and the central image of the prison to give the novel unity; the idea of imprisonment is relevant to every character in the novel.

Language and style

Dickens's use of language in the novel is varied and often striking. The main things to look out for are his use of dialogue and description and the way he manipulates the first-person narrative.

Much of the novel's action takes place through dialogue (conversation) and Dickens often uses it to advance the plot or simply to entertain while revealing his characters. He gets a lot of verbal humor out of Joe, with his mispronunciations and his catchphrases: *"Which I meantersay, Pip, it might be that her meaning here – Make a end on it! As you was! . . . Keep in sunders!"* The same is true for Mrs. Joe, Uncle Pumblechook, and the Aged P. A different effect is apparent with Miss Havisham. Her speech is very theatrical and adds to the sensational tone of the novel: *"When the ruin is complete, and when they lay me dead in my bride's dress on the bride's table . . . so much the better if it is done on this day."* Herbert's fluent, simple, honest speech reveals his frank and generous nature: *"I have been thinking since we have been talking with our feet on this fender, that Estella surely cannot be a condition of your inheritance, if she was never referred to by your guardian."*

The first-person narrative is emotionally intense and very melancholy. Pip's ever-present regret and guilt create a feeling of emotional excess, and the narrative is often highly personal. *Heaven knows we need never be ashamed of our tears, for they are rain upon the blinding dust of earth, overlying our hard hearts*, and *What a doleful night! How anxious, how dismal, how long!*

Often, the simplicity of Pip's statements is what most affects and moves the reader: *I never was happy with her, but always miserable*, and *I never had one hour's happiness in her society*. The constant reiteration of "I" insures that we never forget that this is the painful personal experience of one individual.

Setting and atmosphere

These are vitally important in the novel, and Dickens makes frequent use of description to insure that we respond fully to the novel's different settings. He uses two main geographical locations – Kent and London – and both these settings have key places. The keywords given on p. 31 will help you to get their significance clear in your mind.

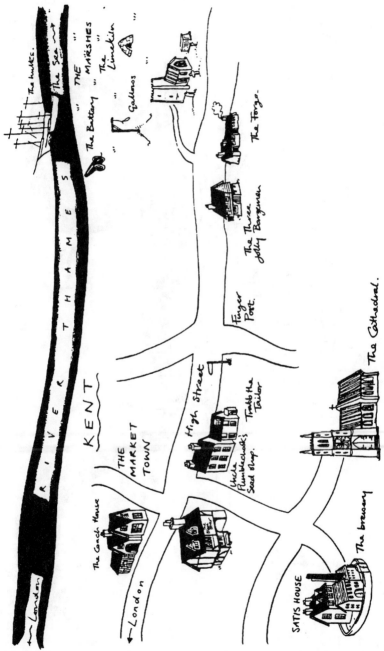

29

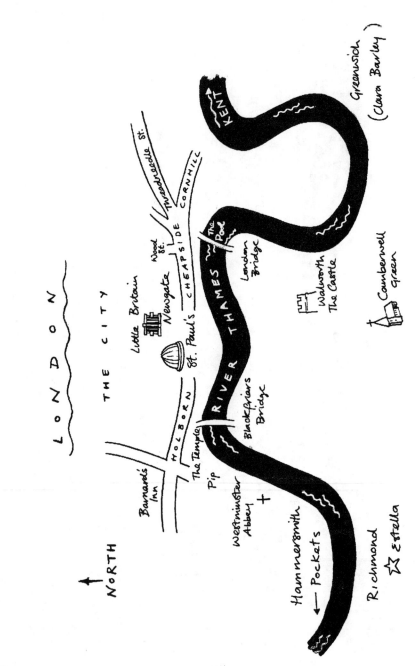

KENT	LONDON
Forge: warmth, love, fire, friendship.	Pip's lodgings: friendship, snobbery, debt.
Marshes: cold, pursuit, convict, dampness.	Newgate: imprisonment, cruelty, injustice, death.
Satis House: bitterness, revenge, death, imprisonment.	Jaggers's offices: death, lack of emotion, greed for power, secrecy.
The limekiln: revenge, hatred, hell.	Wemmick's castle: warmth, friendship, love, suburban values.
	The river: life, death, escape, change.
	Hammersmith: The Pockets
	Richmond: Estella.

The style of description can be simple: *The cold wind seemed to blow colder there,* and *we found a heavy mist out,* and *it fell wet and thick*; elaborate, as in the initial description of Miss Havisham and her room; or sinister and comic at the same time: *a most dismal place; the skylight eccentrically patched like a broken head, and the distorted adjoining houses looking as if they had twisted themselves to peep down at me through it.* Dickens adapts his style according to the effect he is trying to create, and all his references to setting and atmosphere, however brief, are consistent with his purpose.

Imagery

Most of Dickens's imagery is closely linked to his themes and works on a very accessible level. The Mind Map on p. 32 will help you to identify the main groups of images.

now that you're a little more style-conscious, take a break

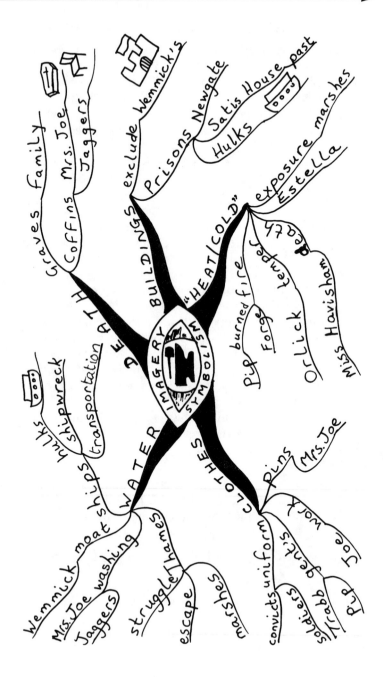

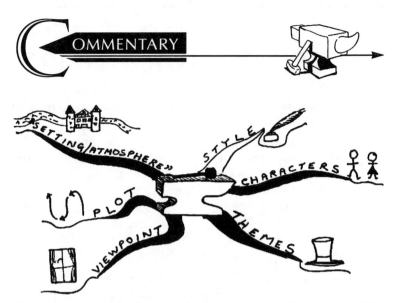

COMMENTARY

The Commentary looks at each chapter in turn, beginning with a brief preview that will prepare you for the chapter and help with reviewing. The Commentary discusses whatever is important in the chapter, focusing on the areas shown in the Mini Mind Map above.

ICONS

Wherever there is a focus on a particular theme, the icon for that theme appears in the margin (see p. xi for key). Look out, too, for the Style and Language icon. Being able to comment on style and language will help you to get an "A" on your exam.

You will learn more from the Commentary if you use it alongside the novel itself. Read a chapter from the novel, then the corresponding Commentary section, or the other way around.

QUESTIONS

Remember that when a question appears in the Commentary with a star ✪ in front of it, you should stop and think about it for a moment. And **do remember to take a break** after completing each exercise.

Chapter 1

- ◆ Pip introduces himself.
- ◆ Pip is wandering in the graveyard when an escaped convict grabs him and threatens him with violence unless he helps him.
- ◆ Pip runs home in terror.

The story is told by the older Pip. The **viewpoint** (the perspective from which the story is told) is that of first-person narrative (*My father's . . . I called myself . . .*). Pip is looking back at his life and examining its key episodes. He is very honest about his faults, and often laughs at himself. Throughout this chapter, and the whole book, everything is seen through Pip's eyes. Here, we share his fear and see all the events from the point of view of a small child.

The theme of death is highlighted immediately as we first see Pip as a lonely orphan walking in a churchyard. The fact that he can only imagine what his family looked like by examining their tombstones is grimly amusing, but it is also an accurate depiction of a child's way of looking at the world. Small children sometimes have difficulty separating reality from fantasy.

Dickens is demonstrating here his fascination with the theme of childhood.

STYLE AND LANGUAGE

Look closely at all the words and phrases that Dickens uses to build up the **setting** (location) and **atmosphere** (mood) of the isolated graveyard: *raw afternoon, this bleak place, dark flat wilderness, distant savage lair.* In the last paragraph of the chapter, he focuses on the *gibbet*, a structure used to hang criminals in early Victorian times. ❍ How do you think he wants his readers to feel at this point?

The **dialogue** (the conversation) between Pip and the convict plays on all our childhood fears and nightmares, but is also rich in dark humor. The convict threatens Pip with a young man who will tear out his heart and liver, and roast and eat them. ❍ Do you think that the "young man" exists? What could be the significance of the convict turning Pip upside down, in relation to what is to follow in the rest of the novel?

Despite his terrifying appearance, *a fearful man, all in coarse grey, with a great iron on his leg*, we cannot help feeling sorry for the convict. This is because Dickens stresses that he is also a man *who limped, and shivered* and *who hugged himself, as if to hold himself together*. Despite all his threats, he has not harmed Pip, so we can already see that his character is complex and intriguing.

Chapter 2

◆ Introduction to characters of Joe Gargery and Mrs. Joe, including physical descriptions.
◆ Mrs. Joe chases Pip with a stick. Joe tries to help Pip by shoving him up the chimney.
◆ Pip hides his supper for the convict.
◆ It's Christmas Eve. Guns are being fired from the convict ships to warn of an escaped prisoner.
◆ Pip is sent to bed because he asks too many questions.
◆ At dawn he steals food from the pantry and a file from Joe's tools for the convict.
◆ He runs out onto the marshes.

 This chapter introduces us to Joe and Mrs. Joe and highlights the themes of guilt, love, and childhood. Dickens's dark humor is evident and the viewpoint of the older Pip is carefully maintained.

Everything Mrs. Joe does is aggressive: She has *a hard and heavy hand*, she throws Pip at Joe (*I often served as a connubial missile*), she cuts the bread angrily, and at one stage Pip says she *knocks Joe's head for a little while against the wall behind him.* When Pip is stirring the Christmas pudding, she attacks him for asking too many questions and packs him off to bed, after giving him (quite pointlessly) with tarwater (a mixture of cold water and tar believed to be a cure-all in Dickens's time).

Her bitter, unpredictable character, which Dickens always treats with grim humor, is strongly contrasted with that of Joe,

 whose behavior often draws our attention to the theme of love. He has a fair, smooth face, curly blond hair, and pale blue eyes. Though physically large and strong, he is also kind, and easygoing. He and Pip have an almost equal relationship, despite the big age difference. Pip treats Joe *as a larger species of child and as no more than my equal.*

❂ What do you think this suggests about Joe's intellect and education? Is Pip right to treat Joe this way?

Joe appears to tolerate Mrs. Joe's constant abuse, though he tries to protect Pip from her. The warmth of his affection for Pip is revealed when Pip tells us how they always used to compare their slices of bread and butter, and suggests that Joe can only enjoy his food if Pip is enjoying his, too.

❂ Can you find another example, later in the chapter, of an action that emphasizes Joe's closeness with Pip, and his fear of his wife?

The theme of guilt runs strongly through the chapter, as the older Pip looks back on his fear and isolation as a child. Dickens stresses his *conscience* and his *guilty knowledge* that he was going to steal from Mrs. Joe. We are aware of the viewpoint of the older Pip when he comments on how terrified children are when they are forced to live with a guilty secret, the first secret in a novel centered on secrecy and mystery. This distances him very starkly from his younger self and suggests his growth from his childhood innocence.

The chapter ends in a frenzy of guilt and fear as Pip runs out from the warmth of the forge into the *misty marshes,* one of the many abrupt changes in setting and atmosphere. This was the end of the first "number" of the novel, which meant that Dickens's original readers had to wait a week to see what happened to Pip, just like a TV program in the twentieth century.

Take a break before the plot thickens

Chapter 3

◆ It's a damp, cold morning when Pip rushes out to see the convict.
◆ He mistakes another convict, also in a prison uniform, for his own convict. This convict tries to hit Pip, but Pip escapes unhurt. Pip thinks he is "the young man."

◆ He meets his own convict, who is very hungry and cold, at the Battery. Pip gives him the food and the file, and tells him about the young man.

◆ Pip runs back to the forge.

The pace of the story escalates in this chapter as the real plot begins to take shape. Our understanding of the rest of the novel depends on our response to this scene and to the relationship between Pip and the convict, Magwitch.

The chapter opens in the damp, eerie atmosphere of the marshes. Everything reminds Pip of his guilt and the whole landscape, animals included, almost seems alive. Dickens does this to confirm Pip's state of extreme terror, which is increased still further by the appearance of the young man, who already has devilish associations for Pip. This is like a scene from a nightmare, when someone we think we know turns out to be a stranger. This reference to a very familiar fear, something we all understand, helps us to identify and sympathize with Pip.

When Pip gives the food to the convict and watches him eat it, Dickens hints at a humanity and sympathy in Pip's attitude that suggests forgiveness of anything the convict has done, and gratitude on the part of the convict. The dialogue suggests this: *Pitying his desolation . . . I made bold to say, "I am glad you enjoy it.". . . "Thankee, my boy. I do."* The convict is no longer frightening, but pitiable. ✪ Can you find three details that make you feel sorry for him?

The dialogue reveals the convict's hatred of the young man and hints at the theme of revenge. Tension is building as we wait for a meeting between the two escaped prisoners. The last glimpse Pip has of the young man reawakens his fear and distrust.

Chapter 4

◆ Christmas dinner at the forge with Pumblechook, Wopsle, and Hubble. All the adults seem to be bullying Pip. Pip's feelings of guilt increase.

◆ Uncle Pumblechook asks for brandy, but spits it, out as Pip has replaced the stolen brandy with tarwater, mistaking it for plain water.

◆ Everything calms down again until Mrs. Joe goes into the pantry to get the pork pie. Pip rushes to the door to escape, straight into a soldier carrying a pair of handcuffs.

This chapter widens the scope of the novel, bringing in a broader range of minor characters. We are aware of Dickens's deep interest in childhood, as he uses the viewpoint of the older Pip to highlight the negligent and unjust treatment of the younger Pip by the adults.

Mrs. Joe's character is given a further dimension when we learn that she is *a very clean housekeeper, but had an exquisite art of making her cleanliness more uncomfortable and unacceptable than dirt itself.* For her, even Christmas Day is miserable, and she also makes it miserable for Joe, who looks *like a scarecrow in good circumstances* in his best church-going clothes, and for Pip, who is unmercifully bullied by the adults at Christmas dinner. Once again, the love and companionship between Pip and Joe is stressed; they even have secret signals, just like friends. ✪ What is the signal that Mrs. Joe is in a bad mood?

The Christmas dinner is rich and elaborate, but the atmosphere is dark, cold, and negative. All the minor characters are eccentric and odd-looking: Mr. Wopsle has a bald, shining head and Roman nose and always sounds like someone in a Shakespeare play, and Uncle Pumblechook is large and slow, *with a mouth like a fish, dull staring eyes, and sandy hair standing upright on his head.* Dickens treats him with sardonic humor, making everything he says sound ridiculous.

PIP'S ANGUISH

 Pip, throughout the chapter, is victimized by the adults, as if he *had insisted on being born.* At dinner, he is not allowed to speak, but the adults direct the conversation at him in a negative and destructive way. ✪ Can you find two other ways in which he is made to feel small and worthless? How does Joe try to cheer him up? They all agree that he has been *a world of trouble* for Mrs. Joe. Dickens's bitterness at this kind of attitude toward children comes over strongly. ✪ How do we know that Pip gets very annoyed by their comments, and particularly by Uncle Pumblechook?

Dickens controls the pace by building up tension, as Pip waits for his theft to be found out. It becomes almost unbearable when Uncle Pumblechook drinks the brandy, then Mrs. Joe goes to the pantry for the pork pie. *I felt that this time I really was gone.* Pip's guilt is so strong that at the end of the chapter he imagines that the handcuffs the soldier is carrying are for him. This is the end of the second magazine installment of the novel, so it is a kind of "cliff-hanger" until the next episode.

Chapter 5

◆ The soldiers are pursuing the convicts, and need a blacksmith to fix the handcuffs.
◆ Mr. Wopsle and Joe, with Pip on his back, join the soldiers in the long hunt for the convicts.
◆ They find both convicts fighting in a ditch. Pip's convict accuses the other man of lying at their trial.
◆ Pip's convict tells the sergeant that he stole the file and food from the blacksmith. Finally, he is rowed out to the prison ship.

Chapter 5 was a "double number," an episode in the story complete in itself. It is one of the novel's most dramatic chapters, full of excitement and pathos. Its central focus is pursuit. For the soldiers, the chase is just a job, and they're looking forward to catching the convicts. But Pip thinks of the convicts as "poor wretches" and tells Joe, *"I hope . . . we shan't find them."*

The hunt itself is carefully paced so that it begins quietly with emphasis on establishing atmosphere. The marshes are *cold and threatening* with *darkness coming on.* Inside the houses are warm, with *glowing windows,* whereas outside there is a *bitter sleet* and an *east wind* and the *shudder of the dying day in every blade of grass.*
✪ How does Dickens remind us again of the opening of the novel? Throughout the pursuit, the tension is intensified by Pip's anxiety that the convict will think it was he who tipped off the soldiers.

The hunt accelerates into a frantic pursuit, ending with the discovery of the convicts. The theme of revenge is present here, as Pip's convict shouts *"Let him go free!"*

and accuses his enemy of lying and cheating. These important hints will be developed later in the story. There is also a suggestion of another theme to be explored, that of class and snobbery, when Pip's convict exclaims bitterly, *"He's a gentleman."*

However, the most important moment in the chapter is when Pip and the convict look into each other's eyes. Pip shakes his head, but the convict doesn't appear to react at all. Of course, the older Pip, with his knowledge of the events that follow, knows the significance of this look, but Dickens keeps us guessing. Otherwise, he would give away the main surprise in the story.

They return the convicts – still unnamed – to the prison ship through the cold and darkness. Joe, like Pip, shows humanity and forgiveness when Magwitch confesses his theft of the pie: *"God knows you're welcome to it . . . we wouldn't have you starved to death for it, poor miserable fellow-creature."* Pip's simple act of kindness (and fear) and the convict's deception to save Pip from punishment create a bond between the two characters on which the whole novel rests.

Now let's recap

?   Think again about Pip's three encounters with the convict. Make a Mini Mind Map of Pip's emotions in all three meetings.

?   Make a Mind Map of Pip's family. You can add to it as you read through the Commentary. Include how Joe and Mrs. Joe treat Pip, and the contrast in their attitudes.

you will shortly meet Miss Havisham – but first take a break

Chapter 6

◆ Pip says he never tells Joe the whole truth for fear of losing his good opinion of him.
◆ Joe carries him home.
◆ Mrs. Joe drags Pip up to bed.

This short chapter simply finishes the chase episode, and insures that we know that Pip never tells Joe the truth about the convict.

 Pip's guilt, secrecy, and dishonesty are stressed further. The older Pip, looking back on and interpreting this episode, realizes the full significance of his failure to tell the truth. The young Pip has a conscience and knows he is doing wrong, but the mature Pip, as narrator, does not let his younger self off: *It was much upon my mind . . . . that I ought to tell Joe the whole truth*, and *I was too cowardly to do what I knew to be right.* He is sharply self-critical when he says that he was *an untaught genius* and learned to do wrong himself, with no one to teach him.

However, the reader can see from the final picture of Pip being dragged up the stairs by his harshly eccentric sister that his childhood has so lacked stability that his insecurity and guilt are very understandable.

Chapter 7

- ◆ Pip is an odd-job boy at the forge prior to his apprenticeship. The money he earns is saved in a money box.
- ◆ Mr. Wopsle's great-aunt runs a village evening school for working children, and a shop, helped by her granddaughter, Biddy. Pip learns his basic alphabet and numbers at the school.
- ◆ We learn of Joe's illiteracy and harsh childhood.
- ◆ Mrs. Joe returns from the market with the news that Miss Havisham wants Pip to go and play at her house.
- ◆ Pip, clean and in a new suit, then goes off with Uncle Pumblechook, who will take him to Miss Havisham the next day.

 This chapter provides a deeper insight into Joe's character and introduces one of the book's most important characters, Miss Havisham. The themes of class and money are further developed.

Pip's uneven education reflects his limited prospects, but Mrs. Joe is still conscious of their "superior position" in the village. Dickens introduces Biddy, a new character, who is an orphan, like Pip.

Joe's childhood, like Pip's, was far from perfect. His father *. . . were given to drink* and drunkenly beat Joe's mother. After a violent life, he died of a *purple leptic fit*. His mother died soon after. Yet Joe is not twisted by this experience and, in fact, seems to have learned from it.

He tells Pip about himself one night as they wait for Mrs. Joe to return from the market with Uncle Pumblechook, and Pip says that he *dated a new admiration of Joe from that night.*

○ Would you have felt the same as Pip?

PIP IS TO MEET MISS HAVISHAM

The last part of the chapter contains details vital to the plot. Dickens gives us a strong impression of the atmosphere in the forge, where it is dry and warm, in contrast to the *dry cold night* where *the wind blew keenly, and the frost was white and hard*. Pip imagines what it would be like to freeze to death out on the marshes. Into this freezing, harsh night, Dickens introduces the character of Miss Havisham.

Although wealthy, she lives in a *dismal house*. Her desire for Pip to come and play seems bizarre.

Uncle Pumblechook, who is her tenant, is proud to have provided the connection with her. However, the ending of the chapter is mournful and low-key, with Pip being dragged away from Joe in an uncomfortable suit, uncertain of what he is supposed to be doing.

Chapter 8

◆ Pip has stayed with Uncle Pumblechook.
◆ Description of Satis House, Miss Havisham, and Estella.
◆ Pip and Estella play cards, then she takes Pip into the yard and gives him food. She makes him cry.
◆ Pip looks around the yard and the deserted brewery. He imagines he sees Miss Havisham hanging from one of the beams.
◆ Estella shows Pip out, and he returns to the forge.

This is one of the most important chapters in the novel, as so much of Pip's suffering comes from his love of Estella, whom we meet here for the first time.

It begins quietly, with a careful description of Uncle Pumblechook's seed and corn shop and the establishment of the slow, leisured atmosphere of the town, where the shopkeepers seem to spend half the day just staring at each other. Pip is glad to say goodbye to Pumblechook, as his *conversation consisted of nothing but arithmetic.*

Dickens builds up to the famous picture of Miss Havisham slowly and carefully. Pip notices that Satis House *was of old brick, and dismal, and had a great many iron bars to it.* "Satis" is Latin for "enough," suggesting a place that is narrow and limited. It's also impossible to ignore the indirect comparison with a prison, linking Estella and her father, Magwitch. Its coldness seems to echo the marshes, *the cold wind seemed to blow colder there,* and the girl who comes to the gate is just as cold. Her name reminds us of the stars (it is Latin for "star"), whose distant cruelty Pip has already observed.

The themes of love, class, and money focus on her, as she first makes Pip aware of his working-class background. She is the same age as Pip, *but beautiful and self-possessed*. She treats Pip with complete contempt.

STYLE AND LANGUAGE

The description of Miss Havisham has many theatrical qualities; the room sounds just like a stage set for a gothic horror play. Throughout the scene, Dickens carefully maintains the viewpoint so that we are aware of how young Pip is and how strange he finds Miss Havisham. Her faded wedding dress, her yellow skin, the boarded-up room, all suggest someone who has been twisted by love. Time has stopped for her at twenty to nine since her heart was broken (Dickens leaves us in suspense as to how) and now she doesn't even know what day it is.

Estella calls Pip *a common laboring boy* and observes *what coarse hands he has*. This is the first time Pip has noticed class differences, and he regrets his upbringing. ✪ How does Estella make him feel when she hands him his food?

 Pip cries bitterly at the pain she causes him. Dickens observes how sensitive children are to injustice.

The last two pages of the chapter confirm again the cold, dead atmosphere. There is nothing living and no activity in the brewery, but wherever Pip looks, he keeps seeing Estella, like a ghost haunting him. His vision of Miss Havisham hanging from a beam is a **foreshadowing** (indirect warning) of what happens later in the book.

Chapter 9

◆ Pressed by Uncle Pumblechook and Mrs. Joe, Pip tells a pack of lies about Miss Havisham.
◆ Joe, Mrs. Joe, and Pumblechook expect Miss Havisham to *do something* for Pip.
◆ In the end, Pip tells Joe the truth.

This chapter stresses the significance and meaning for Pip of his encounter with Miss Havisham. We can already see how meeting her has changed his attitudes.

Dickens's interest in childhood is again shown when he stresses that all children are afraid of being misunderstood. Pip is convinced that if he were to describe Miss Havisham, he would not be understood. The secrecy surrounding Miss Havisham heightens the novel's mystery-thriller structure.

The importance of class in the novel is increasing. Both Mrs. Joe and Pumblechook believe that Miss Havisham will *do something* for Pip. Pip confesses to Joe, in an act of generous honesty that shows his good heart, that *I knew I was common, and that I wished I was not common.* Joe, in turn, shows his love for Pip by providing moral guidance, which Pip later ignores: *If you can't get to be uncommon through going straight, you'll never get to do it through going crooked.* Even so, Pip begins to think *how*

Over to you

? Think again about how class is dealt with in the last few chapters. How do you think Dickens judges Victorian attitudes to class?

? Begin a Mind Map of Miss Havisham. Include her home, her theatricality, and how she relates to – and uses – Pip and Estella. Add to it as you go along.

? Add any new ideas about Joe to your Mind Map of Pip's family.

a birthday and a fight – after the break

Chapter 10

common Estella would consider Joe.

◆ Biddy agrees to help Pip with his studies.
◆ Pip goes to call for Joe at the Three Jolly Bargemen, where

he is sitting with Mr Wopsle and a stranger who stirs his rum and water with a file. The stranger gives Pip a shilling wrapped in two pound notes.

◆ Pip has difficulty sleeping, thinking of the strange man and the convict.

Pip's desire to *get on in life* stems from snobbery and greed. ✪ How do you feel about the way he treats Biddy? Look closely at the description of the school. Find three sentences or phrases that you think are amusing.

Dickens is careful to show us that there is still a connection between Pip and the convict. Pick out three details about the stranger's appearance. ✪ Can we be sure that he knows the convict? How? The gift Pip receives from him reminds us again of the theme of money. Pip's growing snobbery is also highlighted as he thinks *of the guiltily coarse and common thing it was, to be on secret terms of conspiracy with convicts.* His mind is constantly troubled and disturbed: *I*

Chapter 11

screamed myself awake.

◆ Pip visits Miss Havisham. This time Estella takes him to meet some of Miss Havisham's distant relatives. He also meets a man who smells of soap.
◆ When they are alone together, Estella slaps Pip.
◆ Pip walks Miss Havisham around a room with a huge, rotting wedding cake on a table.
◆ The relatives and Estella come up to the room. It is Miss Havisham's birthday.
◆ Estella leaves Pip to eat in the garden. There, he meets a boy who challenges him to a fight. Pip wins convincingly.
◆ Estella allows Pip to kiss her.

Dickens reveals more of the secrets of Miss Havisham's house, and we are introduced to some of her family. The description of the neglected garden and its *cold shadow* reinforces the atmosphere of death surrounding Satis House.

Pip feels that all the people he meets are *toadies and humbug;* most of what they say is very difficult to understand, yet pointless. ✪ Why do you think Dickens makes them so unpleasant? Despite Estella's destructiveness (*she slapped my face with such force as she had*), it is easy to see that Pip will fall in love with her. However, their love will not be a source

 of pleasure: *I was inwardly crying for her then, and I know what I know of the pain she cost me afterwards.*

A MAN SMELLING OF SOAP

Dickens now introduces us to a new character, very important later in the novel. All we know about him is what he looks like, that he has a habit of *biting the side of his great forefinger,* and that he smells of soap. Pip the narrator tells us that he had *no foresight, then, that he ever would be anything to me.* ✪ Why do you think Dickens makes this point?

The theme of death becomes more important in this chapter. Dickens describes the rotting wedding cake in full **gothic** detail (as if in an over-the-top horror movie), and Miss Havisham talks about her birthday and her death as if they are the same thing. The sense of decay has a profound effect on Pip: *I even had an alarming fancy that Estella and I might presently begin to decay.*

Pip's fight with the mysterious young man introduces a new character, significant later in the novel. The episode is treated with humor, and we can't help liking the young man because, as Pip says, he is so *brave and innocent.* Pick out three things that you find amusing about this scene. ✪ Why do you think Estella has a bright flush upon her face when she sees Pip out?

When Pip kisses her, he feels *that the kiss was given to the coarse common boy as a piece of money might have been, and that it was worth nothing.*

Chapter 12

◆ Pip is very worried about having beaten up the young man, but nothing happens because of it.
◆ For eight to ten months, Pip visits Miss Havisham, and often sees Estella.
◆ Pip says nothing to Joe about Satis House.

◆ Miss Havisham tells Pip that it's now time for him to be apprenticed to Joe and that they should bring the *indentures* (the paperwork) to Satis House.

Pip is guiltily anxious about having hurt the young man, but he is never punished. Eight to ten months of the story are summed up, reminding us that the narrator is constantly cutting down his story and focusing on its most important episodes.

Love is again seen as destructive: Miss Havisham tells Estella to *Break their hearts.* The cold and loveless atmosphere cannot fail to influence Pip: *What could I become with these surroundings?* This environment also encourages his secrecy, so that he is unable to talk about Satis House to anyone except Biddy. ❍ How does the older Pip hint to us that Biddy will have an important role later in the story? How does Pip feel about Pumblechook at this point?

Chapter 13

◆ Joe and Pip go to Satis House for Pip to be apprenticed.
◆ Estella takes them up to Miss Havisham, who asks Pip if he wants to be a blacksmith and gives Joe 25 guineas.
◆ Joe gives the money to Mrs. Joe. Pumblechook pretends that he already knew about it.
◆ Pip, now a student-blacksmith, is "bound over" (bonded) at the Town Hall. They celebrate by getting drunk at the Blue Boar.

Pip's developing snobbery makes him ashamed of Joe, and his attitude toward Joe grows harsh as a result. There is a mixture of humor and pathos in the way Joe is presented in this chapter. ❍ Can you find two examples of humor directed at Joe?

We are conscious of the importance of money in the novel when Miss Havisham pays Joe off. ❍ How do we know that she does not intend to give Joe any more money? It is never really Pip's own money, however, as he is only a child, he has very little control over what is happening to him. He is not asked about going out to celebrate, *They were grown up and had their own way.*

Pip's ideas about class are strongly highlighted by the melancholy tone with which the chapter ends.

Now Test yourself

? Make notes on what you have found out so far about Estella, including your feelings about her, in the form of a Mini Mind Map.

? Add notes and thoughts on Biddy to your Mind Map on Pip's family.

? Add any new ideas and further points to your Miss Havisham Mind Map.

Take a break and prepare yourself for a vicious attack

Chapter 14

◆ Pip now thinks of his house as working class and doesn't want to be a blacksmith.
◆ He is worried that one day Estella will look in through the window and see him dirty and working hard.

This chapter underlines Pip's development. Pip isn't shifting all the blame onto Estella and Miss Havisham; he is strongly critical of himself, and bitterly regrets his actions.

He is full of praise for *plain contented Joe.* His memories of Estella bring only restless misery, and his home has lost its special quality. To the Victorians, home was almost a sacred place, so this is like a loss of religious faith.

Chapter 15

◆ Pip decides to visit Miss Havisham, although Joe tries to dissuade him.

◆ Orlick, a workman, is introduced. He quarrels with Mrs. Joe, then fights Joe and loses.
◆ Pip visits Miss Havisham. Estella is abroad.
◆ Pip and Mr. Wopsle go to Pumblechook's house to read a play. They walk back to the forge with Orlick.
◆ Mrs. Joe has been crippled by a hammer blow.

Pip is moving away from Joe emotionally. The older Pip points out that all of his actions at this time were conditioned by acute class consciousness. Although Pip treats Joe like a child, there are a number of indications that he is much sharper than Pip. ❂ What is he afraid that Miss Havisham will think, if Pip visits her? In what sense are his fears confirmed by Pip's dialogue with her in this chapter?

WE MEET ORLICK

Orlick has a vital function in the structure of the novel and appears for the first time here. He is physically strong but *always slouching*. His odd first name, Dolge, separates him from the other characters. The comparisons Dickens makes with him, *like Cain or the Wandering Jew*, increase the impression of darkness and evil. In the Bible story, Cain murdered his brother Abel, and the Wandering Jew was a mythical figure condemned to walk the earth eternally because of his cruelty to Christ when he was carrying his cross. Both these figures are associated with the idea of revenge. Orlick finds it easy to hate people. He hates Pip because he thinks Joe favors him; he hates Mrs. Joe because she flies off the handle with him; he even manages to fight with Joe, although Joe easily floors him. ❂ Does your opinion of Joe change after this?

After the brief comic interlude with Mr. Wopsle, we are once again on the marshes and Dickens's use of setting and atmosphere warns us that a significant event is about to occur. There is a *heavy mist out,* and in the distance they hear the cannon firing from the convict ships. ❂ Can you remember what these ships were called?

The chapter ends with a powerful climax as we find Mrs. Joe injured by *a tremendous blow on the back of the head.*

Chapter 16

◆ Details of Mrs. Joe's assault emerge.
◆ Pip suspects Orlick or the man who showed him the file earlier in the novel.
◆ Mrs. Joe is paralyzed and can't speak. Biddy comes to look after her.
◆ Mrs. Joe identifies Orlick as the culprit by drawing a hammer on her slate.

The role of Orlick is further developed in this chapter. He is a strange and distant character who seems to represent violence and darkness in the novel. ✪ Why is it significant that Mrs. Joe can no longer speak? How does Mrs. Joe's assault highlight the theme of revenge?

Biddy becomes more prominent now, as a permanent part of the household. She will become a significant contrast to Estella as the novel progresses.

Chapter 17

◆ Pip visits Miss Havisham every year on his birthday.
◆ Pip tells Biddy about Estella and about his ambitions.
◆ He is sure that he should be happy and content at the forge, but is unable to get over Estella.

 The chapter expands and deepens the theme of class and accentuates the destructive aspects of love. The dialogue between Pip and Biddy is one of the most important conversations in the book. Throughout, Dickens creates a very delicate balance in our feelings about Pip; although we feel quite repelled by his behavior, he still keeps our sympathy. This is achieved by the use of the first-person narrative. The older Pip hates what he was at this time.

The mention of Pip's annual trips to Miss Havisham reminds us of the source of Pip's discontent. Satis House makes Pip reject his background and origins: *I continued at heart to hate my trade and to be ashamed of home.*

BIDDY IS BETTER?

The close focus on Biddy sharpens our perception of Estella's damaging hold over Pip. Dickens exposes the cold contempt in his attitude to Biddy: *She was common, and could not be like Estella*, yet he indicates that Biddy is a far superior person to Estella. ✪ What are the good, positive qualities in her that we see in this chapter? What do you think of Pip's behavior toward her on their Sunday walk?

Pip's state of mind is presented as being highly confused and ambiguous. He knows that Estella is no good for him: *I thought it would be very good for me if I could get her out of my head.* He also knows that Biddy would be a much better wife, but can only ask, *How could it be, then, that I did not like her much the better of the two?*

However, there is an indication that he has stronger feelings for her than he imagines. ✪ What do you think Dickens is trying to show in his depiction of Pip's attitude to Biddy?

The last two paragraphs in the chapter have a strongly melancholy tone, suggesting that Pip is heading helplessly for disaster. He realizes that Biddy is immeasurably better than Estella and that being a blacksmith is nothing to be ashamed of, but his memories of Estella affect him, *like a destructive missile* constantly disturbing his peace. Love brings not pleasure, but pain and uncertainty.

The chapter ends with an ominous hint that Pip's state of doubt and confusion is about to end abruptly.

Chapter 18

- ◆ Jaggers, a lawyer, meets Joe and Pip at the Three Jolly Bargemen.
- ◆ He tells Pip that he (Pip) is to go to London in one week's time to be educated as "a gentleman." Pip is given 20 guineas for new clothes.
- ◆ Jaggers offers Joe money in compensation but he refuses.

Many of the main themes and plot threads now begin to converge, and the meaning of the novel's title becomes clearer. We are strongly aware of the shaping influence of Pip as narrator, controlling and manipulating our responses to the characters.

The reappearance of Jaggers introduces again the themes of justice and secrecy. Dickens helps us to remember him by repeating his unusual characteristics: his finger biting and the smell of soap. Jaggers also provides a link with Miss Havisham, although, of course, this turns out to be misleading. Think of three adjectives to describe Jaggers's behavior toward Pip and his friends at the Three Jolly Bargemen.

Dickens builds up the tension in this scene by making Jaggers into a powerful and mysterious character, aware of all the secrets of others but giving nothing away himself.

GREAT EXPECTATIONS

The first use of the phrase *great expectations* in the novel is full of irony and hidden meaning. It is possible to expect something you never receive, or, your expectations may be disappointed. Pip's character development throughout the novel focuses on his awareness of how hollow his expectations really are. He also has to learn the true meaning of the word *gentleman*. At this point, being a gentleman is his highest ideal; he associates the idea with Miss Havisham and Estella. He now needs to learn how narrow, constrained, and destructive his definition is.

Even now, there are clues as to the real source of Pip's windfall. The older Pip strongly indicates to the reader that at this stage he lacked vision or insight: "Pip" – the name he must keep – is the name the convict knew him by, and the intention of his benefactor to reveal himself *at first hand by word of mouth* could suggest the desire to make a dramatic return. These details certainly do not point in Miss Havisham's direction, but Pip refuses to see this. He also quickly picks up the name of Matthew Pocket as a relative of Miss Havisham. He is determined to see her influence in everything and is blind to reality.

Dickens insures our sympathy for and support of Joe in this chapter. He is sharply contrasted with Pip in various ways; he is far more suspicious of Jaggers and shows a contempt for the money he offers. The voice of the older Pip, full of suffering and regret, also casts a constant melancholy light on the whole chapter.

The last few pages of the chapter, describing the return to the forge, are among the saddest in the novel. Dickens exposes the cruel arrogance that Pip shows to Joe and Biddy, but still retains at least some of the reader's sympathies by suggesting that Pip *may have been, without quite knowing it, dissatisfied* with himself. He also maintains our emotional attachment to Pip by suggesting the mixture of hope and regret that Pip is feeling. He thinks of his room as a *mean little room,* but it is also *furnished with fresh young remembrances.* Instead of looking forward optimistically to the future, he feels only uneasiness and uncertainty. The chapter's last lines contain a strong sense of innocence lost.

Chapter 19

◆ Pip, now anxious to leave the village, goes for a last walk on the marshes with Joe.
◆ Pip visits Trabb the tailor to get his new clothes, then Uncle Pumblechook for lunch.
◆ Pip says good-bye to Miss Havisham.
◆ Pip leaves early on a Saturday morning.

Already the negative influence of Pip's *great expectations* can be clearly seen. The process of the betrayal of his real friends and the rejection of his origins is well advanced. ✪ What do you find unpleasant about his treatment of Joe in this chapter? What does his conversation with Biddy tell you about her, and about Pip?

There are many indications that the older Pip is disgusted by his younger self and is detaching himself from his former actions. For instance, he is now aware of how patronizing he was toward Joe: *I was not best pleased with Joe's being so mightily secure of me.* He also believes that he can *remove Joe into a higher sphere,* and refers to him as *backward in some things.* He can think, at this stage, only in terms of class and money. Pip's honesty as a narrator insures that we still have some sympathy for him.

PIP FEELS OUT OF PLACE

There is little evidence of hope or optimism in the chapter. Even Pip's clothes are a disappointment. The fact that he feels out of place and uncomfortable in them could imply that he will also be unhappy in his new class. The connection Dickens makes between Pip and Joe confirms this implication, as Pip feels he *was at a personal disadvantage, something like Joe in his Sunday suit.*

 Dickens draws a firm line between the characters who are not tainted by snobbery – Biddy and Joe – and those who are. The biggest snobs in this chapter – Trabb and Pumblechook – are treated with contempt by Dickens and made to look absurd. Their servile attentiveness to Pip is comically grotesque, but it is also a threat to Pip; his tendency to be flattered by their behavior suggests a growing weakness in him.

Similarly, Pip is willing to visit Miss Havisham in his new clothes – thinking that it is her money he is accepting – but he refuses to show himself off in the Blue Boar to please Joe, who has given him not money but unconditional love. The visit itself is undercut with the strongest possible irony. When Pip speaks to Miss Havisham, he believes they are sharing a secret joke about Sarah Pocket. In fact, Miss Havisham is merely using Pip opportunistically to spite her relatives; there is no real connection between her and Pip at all.

Toward the end of the chapter, Pip shows some awareness of the enormity of the step he is taking. Nonetheless, he rejects the love and forgiveness Joe consistently shows him.

He won't even let Joe see him to the coach because he doesn't want Joe to show him up (expose him). The novel is full of wasted opportunities for sharing love, and this is one of them.

The final paragraphs of the chapter hint at loss of innocence and coming tragedy. Pip's tears suggest his hidden conscience and awareness of Joe's love. He is leaving his childhood behind and taking a new step forward: *the mists had all solemnly risen now and the world lay spread before me.*

Try This

? Make a Mini Mind Map of Orlick's role in Chapters 15–17. What do you find interesting about him?

? What are the immediate effects of Pip's good fortune on the Kent characters? Record your impressions in a Mind Map, which you can extend as you go along.

? Begin a Jaggers Mind Map. Record bare details of his role so far and first impressions of his character.

? Add to your Mind Maps of Pip's family and Miss Havisham.

The first section of the novel, focusing on childhood, is now over. The second section will be mostly concerned with class, money and snobbery – but first take a break

Chapter 20

◆ Pip arrives in London.
◆ He takes his first London walk while waiting for Jaggers.
◆ Jaggers tells Pip he's going to live in Barnard's Inn with someone called Herbert Pocket. Pip sets off for his lodgings with Wemmick.

It is appropriate to the novel's general tone of melancholy and disillusionment that Pip's first impressions of London are so depressing. He has *some faint doubts whether it was not rather ugly, crooked, narrow, and dirty.* ✪ What are the three places he sees in this chapter, and what are his impressions of them?

Dickens often uses people's surroundings, particularly their houses and their rooms, to tell us more about their characters. Pick out three details in the description of Jaggers's room that help to create an atmosphere of death and decay.

Outside the room, death is a constant presence. Smithfield market is *all awash with filth and fat and blood and foam* and Pip is shown where the debtors will be hanged in a few days' time, outside Newgate prison. The whole atmosphere is disturbing and corrupt, in sharp contrast to the forge and its warm fire. The corruption extends to Jaggers's treatment of his clients. Money is more important to him than justice. He also seems to enjoy the feeling of power he has over his clients.

Generally, Pip's introduction to London reinforces the darkness surrounding his expectations.

Chapter 21

◆ Wemmick escorts Pip to Barnard's Inn.
◆ Pip's roommate, Herbert Pocket, returns with provisions. Pip recognizes him as the pale young gentleman he fought years before at Miss Havisham's.

Barnard's Inn is also associated with decay and disillusionment. Pick out three words or phrases from the description of the buildings that you think are effective.

Wemmick, a bachelor of 40 to 50 years old, is a true Londoner, and at first he seems very dry and unemotional to Pip. ❂ What details of his behavior or appearance suggest this lack of emotion? Is there anything comic in the description?

Dickens treats Herbert's meeting with Pip with light and affectionate humor, but there are serious undertones: Herbert provides a misleading link with Miss Havisham, and he is someone Pip never expected to see again.

Pip decides at the end of the chapter that London is decidedly overrated.

Chapter 22

◆ Over lunch, Pip tells Herbert his story and asks him to advise him on his manners.
◆ Herbert tells Pip Miss Havisham's story.

◆ Herbert is looking for an opening in insurance at the moment and is not very well off.
◆ Herbert and Pip do some sightseeing. They visit Herbert's father and his chaotic family in Hammersmith.

Herbert Pocket is one of the characters we learn to trust the most, and Dickens immediately stresses his openness and good humor. He has *a frank and easy way with him* and *a natural incapacity to do anything secret and mean.* He is also (like many of Dickens's characters) eccentric, calling Pip *Handel* after the composer of a piece of music called "The Harmonious Blacksmith." However, the delicate way he advises Pip on his manners suggests that he may be more intelligent than he appears. ✪ What does Pip think about Herbert's financial prospects?

Dickens needs to keep the different threads of the plot going, which is one of the reasons why Herbert tells Pip Miss Havisham's story in this chapter. There are loose ends: Estella's origins, the whereabouts of Miss Havisham's lover and her half-brother, and these arouse curiosity and maintain suspense. The story also reveals that Estella is part of Miss Havisham's plot to get revenge on all men because of her unhappy experience in love. Class is relevant to Miss Havisham's story, too, as her father was a gentleman brewer, while her lover was clearly from a lower social class.

Pip can't help noticing that Herbert accepts his relative poverty cheerfully. Pip is already becoming a greedy snob, leaving Joe and Biddy far behind. His strongest feelings are of guilt and loneliness: *in the London streets, so crowded with people and so brilliantly lighted in the dusk of evening, there were depressing hints of reproaches for that I had put the poor old kitchen at home so far away.*

Chapter 23

◆ Background to the Pockets.
◆ The other students in the house taught by Matthew Pocket are called Drummle and Startop.
◆ Dinner at the house described.

The scenes with the Pocket family provide the welcome relief of humor in a novel that can often seem dark and melancholy. The scene at the dinner table is full of straightforward farcical comedy focused on the inefficiency of the Pockets as parents.

 The description of Mrs. Pocket **satirizes** (critically ridicules) Victorian snobbishness.

 The Pocket children expand, again humorously, the theme of childhood. Like so many children in Dickens's novels, they are neglected and forgotten.

Two new characters, Drummle and Startop, are introduced. Drummle has an important function later in the novel. He is described as *sulky* and *heavy*.

Looking back

? Jot down all the names of the places in London that Pip has visited so far. Locate them on the map of London (p. 30). Briefly review his first impressions of all the London settings. See if you can sketch the map from memory.

? Test yourself on Miss Havisham's story. Draw key images to help you remember it.

? Jot down the names of new characters introduced in Chapters 20–23.

before you learn more about Jaggers, take a break

Chapter 24

◆ Pip's education with Mr. Pocket is mainly concerned with manners and behavior. He is not being trained for a profession.
◆ Pip asks Jaggers for £20 to furnish his room.
◆ Wemmick shows him around Jaggers's office and invites Pip to his house.

Jaggers is a threatening presence, frequently associated with macabre imagery. The focus on secrecy reinforces this negative impression. Dickens uses his possessions and his surroundings to describe him. For instance, his boots seem to be part of him,  *he sometimes caused the boots to creak, as if they laughed in a dry and suspicious way.* When Wemmick reveals to Pip the stories behind the plaster casts on the walls, we are even more aware of the complexity of Jaggers's character. We don't know what his relationship with the criminals was, only that he is motivated by money and not justice. Pip comments: *which side he was on, I couldn't make out.*

Wemmick introduces another mysterious element in the novel when he refers to Jaggers's housekeeper as *a wild beast tamed.* She is very important later in the novel. At the moment, Dickens is creating tension and arousing our curiosity.

Chapter 25

◆ Bentley Drummle and Startop described.
◆ Herbert now Pip's closest friend.
◆ Pip has dinner with Wemmick at the "castle" at Walworth, and meets Wemmick's father.

This chapter gives more information about Wemmick's character and indirectly throws more light on Jaggers.

Wemmick's house tells you a great deal about him. Its neatness and cleanliness reveal a domestic side to him. ❂ What does his behavior toward the "Aged P" show about him? The eccentricities – the flagpole and drawbridge, the gun going off at 9.00 P.M., and the pig in the garden – provide comic relief. Remember that this is an ordinary suburban semi-attached house. Wemmick calls it a castle because that's how he thinks of it.

Chapter 26

◆ Pip has dinner with Jaggers in Soho. Drummle, Startop, and Herbert are also present.
◆ Pip notices Jaggers's housekeeper, Molly, and Jaggers gets her to show off her wrists.
◆ They all get rather drunk and Startop and Drummle quarrel. Jaggers takes a liking to Drummle.

This chapter focuses firmly on Jaggers. He becomes more sinister when Dickens describes his constant hand washing. It is as if he is trying to wash all the corruption away. Later in the novel, he also washes his hands of Pip's misunderstandings. The parallel with Pontius Pilate, who washed his hands of Jesus Christ, leaving him to the mercy of the crowd, is obvious and very disturbing. Like his office, his house is unsettling, *in want of painting, and with dirty windows.*

Jaggers's housekeeper is an important character in the novel, although we see her only briefly here. Dickens makes sure that we remember her by describing her as *like the faces I had seen rise out of the witches cauldron* at a production of Macbeth. (Jaggers's hand washing is like Lady Macbeth's.)

When Jaggers shows his guests Molly's wrists, we feel unnerved by his behavior, and also curious about who she is and where she has come from.

Jaggers likes Drummle but warns Pip to *Keep as clear of him as you can.* Pip detests Drummle, and because we see him through Pip's eyes, we dislike him, too. ✪ Why do you think Jaggers likes him?

Chapter 27

◆ A letter from Biddy tells Pip that Joe is coming to London with Mr. Wopsle.
◆ Joe comes to breakfast with Pip and Herbert. He is uncomfortable and behaves in an embarrassing way.
◆ Joe tells Pip that Estella has come back to Satis House and wants to see him.

The chapter balances Pip's snobbery against Joe's love. Read Biddy's letter carefully. ✪ How do we know from reading it that they have not forgotten Pip as he has forgotten them?

Dickens uses the narrative to explore Pip's feelings as honestly as possible. Pip says he will *confess* his feelings.
✪ What are they? Write down three points.

Joe does a number of things that could be seen as embarrassing or laughable. Jot down two things that particularly annoy Pip. However, he is very perceptive about London (remember that Pip, too, was very disappointed by his first impressions). He says of Barnard's Inn that *I wouldn't keep a pig in it myself.*

Joe's message from Miss Havisham moves the plot along and prepares us for a move back to the novel's other main setting, the forge in Kent.

The chapter ends with a note of regret, as Pip runs out after Joe leaves, but fails to catch him. Compare with Chapter 20.
❍ What are the similarities between these scenes?

Gather your thoughts

? How has Pip changed since his arrival in London?
? Think about Joe. Jot down as many adjectives as you can think of to describe him and locate useful quotes from his speeches in the last few chapters.
? Add to your Jaggers Mind Map.

Take a break before Pip sets off for Kent

Chapter 28

◆ Pip sets off for Kent in the same coach as two convicts, one of whom Pip recognizes as the man with the file.
◆ The man doesn't recognize Pip now. Pip overhears the convicts talking. The man he recognizes tells the other how Magwitch told him to find Pip and give him the two one-pound notes as thanks for helping him.
◆ Pip arrives in his village and settles in at the Blue Boar.

 The older Pip is completely honest about his callousness in deciding not to stay at the forge; his sense of social superiority overtakes him at this time. The presence of the convicts on the coach brings back painful memories for Pip. The improbability of this event reminds us of the sensation-novel structure. Dickens abandons realism whenever he needs to.

STYLE AND LANGUAGE

Dickens gives a strong impression of atmosphere as the coach approaches the village. It is miserably raw and Pip senses *marsh country in the cold damp wind that blew at us*. We are filled with foreboding as to what is going to happen. The convicts also help to remind us about what happened to Pip; we are never allowed to forget his early meeting with Magwitch.

The fear that unexpectedly engulfs Pip stems from the irrational guilt of childhood and suggests a central unsolved mystery at the heart of the novel. *I could not have said what I was afraid of, for my fear was altogether undefined and vague, but there was great fear upon me.*

Chapter 29

◆ Pip visits Miss Havisham. Orlick is now the porter at Satis House, which is unchanged.

◆ Estella is older and more beautiful.

◆ Jaggers joins them for dinner.

◆ Pip stays overnight at the Blue Boar and returns home without seeing Joe.

This is one of the most important chapters in the novel. The main focus is on love and class, but the chapter's real interest lies in the fact that the older Pip is holding back information from the reader to increase the suspense and to intensify the irony later on in the book. Dickens's handling of the narrative here is magnificent.

The younger Pip is constantly misinterpreting and misunderstanding Miss Havisham and her intentions for Pip and Estella. He is convinced that *it could not fail to be her intention to bring us together*. His experience of love is also highly negative, giving the chapter a tragic feel. Pick out the words and phrases that suggest this negativity.

Pip's return visit to Miss Havisham is full of the past. When he wheels her around he says: *It was like pushing the chair itself back into the past.* For him, Estella represents everything he wants to be: *I slipped hopelessly back into the coarse and common boy again.* She has money, wealth, and gentility, as he thinks. It is Estella who has made him *ashamed of home and Joe.* In other words, she has caused him suffering and pain and taught him prejudice, yet he cannot separate her from his *innermost life.* Dickens constantly stresses her coldness and hardness. She says to Pip, *"I have no heart – if that has anything to do with my memory."* The irony here, of course, is that in warning Pip of her own coldness, Estella is betraying a warmth of feeling that tells us that she does have a heart, however Miss Havisham has twisted her.

Dickens also creates a feeling of mystery around Estella when he describes the strange sensation Pip has when looking at her that he has *seen a ghost. "What was it?"* Of course, the narrator Pip knows the reality that Estella is, in fact, the illegitimate child of Molly (Jaggers's housekeeper) and Magwitch, but the truth would ruin the steady development of the plot. So Dickens tickles our curiosity by these obvious hints: An attentive reader might make the connection. Did you?

Jaggers once again surfaces as a key character. He obviously knows all about Estella's background, but is deliberately allowing Pip to be misled. Find an example of this deliberate mischief. Significantly, he avoids direct contact with Estella and never looks at her. Pip dislikes seeing him in close contact with her.

The chapter ends with a note of negativity and guilt; Pip is aware of how wrong his behavior is, but is unable to stop himself.

Chapter 30

- ◆ Pip returns home after briefly bumping into Trabb's boy.
- ◆ Pip opens his heart to Herbert about Estella. Herbert is engaged to Clara Barley.
- ◆ Herbert and Pip go out and see Mr. Wopsle in *Hamlet* at a small theater in London.

The main themes of this chapter are again love and class. Pip's new position doesn't fool everyone; Trabb's boy is just as rude as ever to him. However, Pip's snobbery stops him from going to see Joe, so he sends *a penitential codfish and a barrel of oysters*.

Herbert shows his friendship for Pip by trying to advise him on Estella, but the dialogue only confirms Pip's obsession: *"You can't detach yourself?" "No. Impossible!"* The chapter is also full of warnings. Pip observes, *I know I have done nothing to raise myself in life, and that Fortune alone has raised me*. Fortune could just as easily let him down. Herbert also warns Pip that *Estella surely cannot be a condition of your inheritance, if she was never referred to by your guardian*. As when Joe, much earlier, advised Pip not to go and visit Miss Havisham, we feel that Pip is choosing to ignore good advice.

Chapter 31

◆ Pip and Herbert go to see Mr. Wopsle playing Hamlet. He goes back to Barnard's Inn with them for dinner.

The chapter provides a brief comic break, focusing on a very bad production of the famous Shakespearean tragedy. Mr. Wopsle reminds us of Pip's humble past.

When Wopsle goes to supper with Pip and Herbert, he seems a very pitiful figure and it depresses Pip.

Test yourself

? How has Herbert shown his friendship for Pip in these chapters?

? Remind yourself of who the men on the coach are. Memorize the basic details of this scene by trying to picture it in your mind's eye.

? Add any ideas about Estella's effect on Pip to your Estella Mind Map.

a trip to prison, and a death in the family – after the break

Chapter 32

- ◆ A letter from Estella informs Pip that she is coming to London.
- ◆ Pip arrives at the coach station very early to meet her and bumps into Wemmick, who shows him around Newgate prison.
- ◆ He meets the coach.

This chapter is full of irony. The pain that love causes Pip is stressed when he reads Estella's letter. *My appetite vanished instantly, and I knew not peace or rest until the day arrived.*

The tour of the prison prepares us for the unraveling of the mystery surrounding Estella. Pip is horrified by the dark atmosphere of Newgate, *a frouzy, ugly, disorderly, depressing scene it was*, and is disgusted that he allowed himself to be shown around. He feels that he is somehow polluting himself. Look closely at the last two paragraphs of the chapter. ❍ In what way is Pip completely wrong about Estella and the prison? What is the nameless shadow he sees when she waves from the coach? Do you think these tantalizing hints work?

Chapter 33

- ◆ Estella and Pip have tea and talk, then Pip drives her to a house in Richmond where she is going to stay with a lady and her daughter.
- ◆ Pip returns to the Pockets's house in Hammersmith.

In this chapter, Dickens establishes a connection between Jaggers and Estella. The chapter also confirms Pip's obsession with Estella and stresses its negative effect. Pick out three phrases or sentences in the chapter that suggest this negativity.

Chapter 34

- ◆ Pip and Herbert are getting heavily into debt. Not very happy.
- ◆ Pip receives a letter from Biddy saying Mrs. Joe has died.

The chapter confirms the feeling of gloom surrounding Pip's money and his expectations. It also reveals his guilt: *I lived in a state of chronic uneasiness respecting my behavior to Joe.* For the first time, he suggests that it would have been better if he had never met Miss Havisham, *and had risen to manhood content to be partners with Joe in the honest old forge.* The coldness of Pip's wealth and of Estella is contrasted with the warmth of the forge.

The pointless extravagance and the corruption of Herbert stresses how far-reaching the destructiveness of Pip's money is; at the end of the chapter, the letter comes as a dramatic reminder of everything Pip has rejected, and highlights the triviality of his own life. It also focuses the reader's mind on the theme of death.

Chapter 35

◆ Pip returns to Kent for the funeral.
◆ He stays at the forge, and talks to Biddy after dinner about Mrs. Joe's death and about Orlick.

The effect of the death on Pip is sobering and dramatic. When he returns to his old village, he can't help thinking of his own death and hopes that he will be sympathetically remembered. The funeral itself has many touches of dark humor but the final impression is of peace and rest.

The dialogue between Pip and Biddy reminds us of his cruelty in abandoning them all. He has even made them feel embarrassed about their manners. Biddy's description of Mrs. Joe's death is unexpectedly moving. ✪ What do you think was in Mrs. Joe's mind when she died? The last part of the chapter makes us very clearly aware of the older Pip's looking back with guilt on his treatment of Joe and seeing how far Joe was superior to him. Find two examples of this attitude to Joe in this chapter.

Pip is honest about the fact that he will not visit the forge again, stressing that he still has a long way to go in his development.

Think again

? Compare the behavior of Estella and Biddy in Chapters 32–35. Compare Pip's behavior toward them. ✪ How do you feel about it? Record your ideas on the chart below

ESTELLA   **BIDDY**

<------------------------PIP------------------------->

? Think about the significance of Newgate in the novel. Why do you think Pip is so disturbed by prisons, prisoners, and criminals?

Take a break before Pip meets his benefactor

Chapter 36

◆ Pip is now 21. He goes to see Jaggers, who gives him £500 as his annual income.
◆ He refuses to give away any secrets about who is sending Pip the money.
◆ Jaggers goes to dinner with Pip and Herbert.

Pip's expectations seem more real when we are told the exact amount of money he is being paid. Jaggers seems to be enjoying the power his secrets give him over Pip, and continues to mislead Pip about Miss Havisham.

Pip's twenty-first birthday dinner is very gloomy and depressing, due to Jaggers's presence. Jaggers casts a shadow wherever he is, throughout the novel, and is a focus of secrecy and mystery.

Chapter 37

- ◆ Pip visits Wemmick and his father at "The Castle" in Walworth for tea and meets Miss Skiffins.
- ◆ He asks Wemmick's advice on how to help Herbert financially.
- ◆ After a few weeks, he manages to set Herbert up in business, with a shipping broker, Clarriker. Herbert has no idea who has set him up.

At last, some good is coming from Pip's money. A combination of love, guilt, and his natural kindness inspire him to set something up for Herbert. The theme of mystery is highlighted as, like Pip himself, Herbert never knows where his good fortune comes from. ❂ Why do you think Pip cries at the end of the chapter?

Dickens constantly stresses that there is a big difference between Wemmick's work and home life. ❂ In what way is he so different at home?

The last paragraph of the chapter is a cliff-hanger, warning us that a big shock is coming that is related to the novel's central mystery. This technique reminds us that this is not a realistic novel. Dickens is using the format of the sensational novel so popular in Victorian times.

Chapter 38

- ◆ Pip often spends time with Estella, who is living at Richmond.
- ◆ They visit Satis House. Pip stays the night there for the first time.
- ◆ Estella flirts with Bentley Drummle at a ball in Richmond.

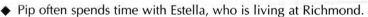

Pip remains obsessed with Estella, but the love he feels is always associated with pain. We read that he *suffered every kind and degree of torture that Estella could cause,* and that he *never had one hour's happiness in her society.*

Satis House is still the same, but now Miss Havisham seems even crazier and Pip is more disgusted by her. He doesn't see anything glamorous about Satis House anymore, but sees it as a *darkened and unhealthy house in which her life was hidden from the sun*. She seems more ghostlike than ever. Pip describes her as *a very spectre* and he sees her haunting the corridors of the house when he tries to sleep, yet he still clings to the belief that she has given him his expectations and that Estella is part of them.

Pip observes that *Estella was set to wreak Miss Havisham's revenge on men*, but Miss Havisham may be having second thoughts. ● What do you think her feelings are?

Bentley Drummle is also just as revolting as ever, but very successful in his attentions to Estella: *The Spider, doggedly watching Estella, outwatched many brighter insects.*

The last paragraph of the chapter is another cliff-hanger, hinting, again, that a bombshell is about to change Pip's life.

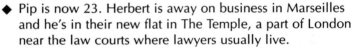

Chapter 39

◆ Pip is now 23. Herbert is away on business in Marseilles and he's in their new flat in The Temple, a part of London near the law courts where lawyers usually live.

◆ It's a stormy night. A stranger appears on Pip's staircase and reveals himself as Abel Magwitch, Pip's convict, and his mysterious benefactor.

◆ After finding out that the convict will probably be executed if he's found, Pip lets him stay in Herbert's room. He hardly sleeps that night.

STYLE AND LANGUAGE

This is possibly the most important chapter in the book, memorable for its drama and emotion. It is full of imagery of shipwreck, loss, and death, and focuses on the sudden and violent collapse of Pip's expectations as the source of his fortune is revealed to be the convict of the first chapter. All his dreams and plans have come to nothing.

Dickens uses setting and atmosphere to intensify feeling throughout the chapter. It begins in storm and tempest, as if the violent weather is giving Pip a premonition of the storm that is about to break in his life. The city is dirty, *mud, mud, mud, deep in all the streets*, and Pip, in his room high above the Thames, feels as if he is *in a storm-beaten lighthouse*. He hears rumors from the coast *of shipwreck and death*. All the images of water and the sea create a link with the watery marsh country where he first met the convict.

What happens next?

Tension builds up, accentuated by the striking clocks as Pip stops reading. The whole process of recognition of the convict is presented with agonizing slowness. First, he walks up the dark staircase into the light, when we get a clear visual picture of him. Pip doesn't recognize him until he says, *"You're a game one,"* and the recognition comes suddenly and violently. All the time, the convict is behaving with great affection and tenderness toward Pip.

Pip is at first cold to the convict. As the convict questions him on where his money comes from, by an elaborate guessing game, Pip at last realizes that, in fact, this is his benefactor: *All the truth of my position came flashing on me.*

71

● Why do you think Pip is so unwelcoming to Magwitch, and so horrified by him? What's your opinion about the way Magwitch has behaved?

Pip's immediate response is to wish that he had never met him, *O that* [Jaggers] *had never come! That he had left me at the forge – far from contented, yet, by comparison, happy!* ● At this stage, do you agree with Pip? Would he have been better off without his money?

Once the convict has gone to bed, Pip has time to think through the implications of what has happened. He feels bound to Magwitch by *gold and silver chains* and knows that Magwitch's life depends on him, yet he shrinks from him *with the strongest repugnance.* ● Finally, Pip pictures his whole dilemma in one very powerful image—what is it?

In his utter disillusionment, he now realizes that all his dreams about Miss Havisham and Estella were a complete fantasy and that he has deserted Joe not for a higher class, but for the convict. Guilt and regret rush in upon him: *I could never, never, never, undo what I had done.* ● What are your feelings toward Pip now? Would you have felt the same as he?

Now look back

? How has Miss Havisham changed since we last saw her?

? Jot down as many adjectives as you can think of to describe the convict. Add some of them to your "convict" Mind Map.

? Try writing or speaking out loud Magwitch's account of his meeting with Pip.

The mystery unravels – but first take a break

Chapter 40

◆ Pip tells his servant that his uncle has come to visit him. He trips over a man asleep on the stairs, who is not there when he gets back with the night watchman, who says that he saw someone following Pip.

◆ Magwitch (Provis in Australia) has breakfast with Pip.
◆ Pip visits Jaggers, who confirms the truth of Magwitch's revelations.
◆ Pip buys Magwitch clothes.
◆ Herbert returns after Magwitch has been staying for five days.

The presence of the sleeping stranger adds a further element to the novel's mystery. Pip is in a kind of dream, unable to come to terms with what has happened. He feels *chained* to the convict (note Dickens's constant use of prison imagery) but he disgusts Pip, and new clothes make him look even worse. *The more I dressed him . . . the more he looked like the slouching fugitive on the marshes.* Dickens is suggesting that class cannot be bought with money; what you really are will always come out. (Compare Joe in his best clothes.)

The scene with Jaggers reminds us of how corrupt he is. He has let Pip believe that Miss Havisham was his benefactor, but now says, *"I am not at all responsible for that."* ❸ Do you think he is?

Herbert's arrival is a real relief. His *airy freshness* lightens the atmosphere of gloom and sadness. Pip can always rely on unquestioning love and friendship from a number of characters in the novel. ❸ Who are they?

Chapter 41

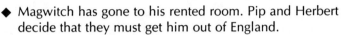

◆ Magwitch has gone to his rented room. Pip and Herbert decide that they must get him out of England.
◆ The next morning, they ask Magwitch to tell them about the other convict he fought with on the marshes.

Pip's friendship with Herbert helps him to fight the terror and disgust overwhelming him. Herbert is also horrified and anxious to get the convict out of danger. Pip thinks of how his dreams have come to nothing, and of how useless his life now seems: *I have been bred to no calling, and I am fit for nothing.*

Herbert reminds Pip that Magwitch, too, has had *great expectations*. He has come to England to realize his *fixed idea* and if he is disappointed, will become violent. Pip must not *cut the ground from under his feet*.

Chapter 42

◆ Magwitch tells his life story. He was an orphan, and grew up as a young criminal. He met Compeyson (who was in business with someone called Arthur) and joined him in his forgery business, eventually being caught, tried, and transported to Australia.

◆ Herbert passes Pip a note, telling him that Arthur was Miss Havisham's half-brother's name, and that it was Compeyson who broke her heart.

All the plot lines now begin to come together. Compeyson focuses the novel's themes of class, money, love, and revenge; he is a central character, though we hardly see him. His hardness and cruelty (*no more heart than an iron file*) link him to Estella. His class background makes it possible from him to escape justice while Arthur goes mad through guilt, hallucinating about Miss Havisham. The idea of childhood is also revived, briefly, in Magwitch's description of how he grew up.

Like Pip, Magwitch is at a disadvantage because of his class. He is helpless against Compeyson and against the legal system that makes justice impossible. Pip admits that he *had felt great pity for him*. ✪ How do you feel about Magwitch now?

The note at the end of the chapter confirms what we had already guessed: that Magwitch and Miss Havisham are linked, though apparently indirectly, through Compeyson.

Chapter 43

◆ Pip decides to go to Satis House to see Estella and Miss Havisham.

◆ He meets Bentley at the Blue Boar and they nearly fight.

Pip is obsessed with *the abyss between Estella in her pride and beauty*, and Magwitch. This is ironic, as Pip doesn't yet realize the link between the young woman and the convict.

He is now fully aware of the viciousness of his behavior to Joe: *I was capable of almost any meanness towards Joe or his name.* He also accepts that everything to do with Satis House has been a mistake: *it would have been so much the better for me never to have entered it.*

Chapter 44

◆ Pip visits Miss Havisham and Estella.
◆ He asks Miss Havisham to help Herbert by continuing to supply him with money.
◆ He confesses his love to Estella and begs her not to marry Drummle, but she is unmoved.

The changes that Pip's disillusionment have made in his life are now very obvious. Satis House now seems *a natural place* for him. Setting and atmosphere reflect his feelings.

Just as he accused Jaggers of misleading him, he now accuses Miss Havisham. She, too, denies responsibility: *You made your own snares.* ✪ Again, what do you think?

✪ What does Pip's confession of love for Estella reveal about her? How does Miss Havisham react to their behavior? What do you think she is feeling? The themes of money and revenge are highlighted; Miss Havisham is taking revenge on her greedy relatives as well as on men.

The chapter ends with another cliff-hanger, leaving us in suspense. Wemmick's note clearly suggests danger, but we have to wait to discover what that danger is.

Try this

❓ Complete the diagram on p. 76 of the novel's female characters by connecting those who are linked and adding details of each woman's effect on Pip.

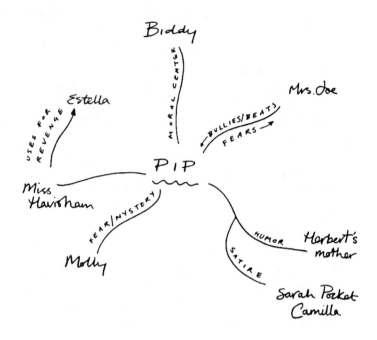

Biddy

MORAL CENTER

Estella

USES FOR REVENGE

Mrs. Joe

BULLIES/BEATS
FEARS →

PIP

Miss
Havisham

FEAR/MYSTERY

Molly

HUMOR   Herbert's
mother

SATIRE

Sarah Pocket
Camilla

Chapter 45

◆ Pip spends a disturbed night at The Hummums, a seedy hotel in London's Covent Garden.
◆ Wemmick tells Pip that Pip's lodgings are being watched and that Compeyson is alive and in London.
◆ While Pip was in Kent, Wemmick and Herbert arranged to move Magwitch to Herbert's girlfriend's house near Greenwich (in Docklands) for safety.

We are now firmly into the medium of the "sensational" novel: fast-paced, gothic, and full of twists and turns. The Hummums is a suitably nasty setting for Pip's restless, fearful night. Appropriately, too, for a mystery novel, we have a lot of plotting and secrecy.

Compeyson's presence in London is another development of the theme of pursuit. In this chapter, Dickens is laying down foundations for the final chase sequence, with Magwitch as the victim.

Chapter 46

- Pip installs Magwitch safely in Clara Barley's house where she lives with her drunken father.
- Herbert and Pip have a plan for Pip to row up and down the river regularly before Magwitch's escape. Magwitch will pull down the blind if all is well.
- They put the plan into action.

We can pause to take a breath in this chapter. Dickens lessens the tension for a while by giving us a few touches of his usual black humor in Bill Barley (yet another Dickensian eccentric). He also gives us a picture of real tenderness and affection in Clara and Herbert. Their love makes Pip feel even more lonely, *I thought of Estella, and of our parting, and went home very sadly*. Herbert and Clara represent normal, healthy love, unlike the destructive love Pip has for Estella.

Pip's feelings toward the convict are now changing. ✪ Why do you think this is happening? He feels that Magwitch is *softened* and admits that *I little supposed my heart could ever be as heavy and anxious at parting from him as it was now.*

The theme of pursuit is now beginning to take over as the pace of the novel accelerates. Pip constantly feels he is being watched and feels that the river is flowing toward Magwitch and that *any black mark on its surface might be his pursuers, going swiftly, silently, and surely, to take him.*

Chapter 47

- Weeks pass quietly. Pip gets deeper into debt.
- Pip visits the theater to see Mr. Wopsle in a bad play and pantomime.
- Afterwards, Wopsle tells him that one of the convicts from the marshes was sitting behind him at the play.

Pip's increasing debt stresses the collapse of his expectations. Tension builds up: *I waited, waited, waited.* The comic interval with Wopsle only heightens the shock we feel when he asks Pip *"But who else was there?"* Later he adds: *"One of those two prisoners sat behind you tonight. I saw him over your shoulder."* We realize that Pip's   77 sensation of being watched and followed was, in fact, quite justified. The description of Compeyson sitting *like a ghost* also captures perfectly the haunted atmosphere of the novel, where nothing is ever really left behind, and no action or word is without consequences. Compeyson – and the past – are catching up!

Chapter 48

◆ Pip has dinner with Jaggers and Wemmick.
◆ They discuss Estella. Suddenly, something about the housekeeper, Molly, convinces Pip that she is Estella's mother. Walking home with Pip, Wemmick tells him Molly's story.

More and more of the story's mysteries are now being uncovered. Once again, Jaggers seems to know all the secrets, but keeps them to himself. Pip's realization that Molly is Estella's mother comes suddenly and dramatically, like all the novel's revelations: *her hands were Estella's hands, and her eyes were Estella's eyes.* It's easy, here, to recognize the use of "sensational" techniques.

The story of her marriage to a *tramping man* brings her closer to Magwitch in the reader's mind, but Pip still does not make the connection.

Look back again

? Add to your Jaggers and Magwitch Mind Maps.
? Jot down the different types of pursuit featured in these four chapters.

Time for a break before the final pieces of the puzzle fall into place

Chapter 49

◆ Pip visits Miss Havisham. She gives Pip £900.
◆ Miss Havisham feels guilty about what she has done to Pip and Estella. She begs Pip's forgiveness.

- Pip confirms that Jaggers brought Estella to Miss Havisham when she was about three years old.
- As Pip is leaving, he looks into Miss Havisham's room just as her dress catches fire. He tries to save her and badly burns his own hands.
- He leaves the next day, whispering to her that he forgives her.

The focus of the novel is now fully on Pip. His view of life is colored with melancholy disillusionment and his growth is almost complete. When he returns to his hometown, he seeks *to get into the town quietly by the unfrequented ways.* He observes that *the cathedral chimes had at once a sadder and more remote sound to me and the place was changed, and. . . Estella was gone out of it for ever.* He also confesses to Miss Havisham that his life has been *a blind and thankless one.*

His relationship with Miss Havisham has changed completely. He pities her *utter loneliness* (perhaps because he himself is so acutely lonely). ❂ How does she show her regret for what she has done, both in her actions and in her words? If you had been Pip, would *you* have forgiven her? What are your reasons?

This is Miss Havisham's last chapter, and it's full of the gothic horror we usually associate with her. Pip has a *presentiment that I should never be there again* and says *I fancied that I saw Miss Havisham hanging to the beam.* The fire that finally consumes her – symbolic of the fires of love, revenge, and guilt – seems to bring the novel nearer to its final conclusion. She is at last lying where Pip had heard her say that she would lie one day. Pip's gesture of forgiveness closes the chapter and also closes this stage of his life.

Chapter 50

- Pip has been quite badly injured by the fire. Herbert looks after him.
- Herbert tells Pip more of Magwitch's story. He was once connected with a *revengeful woman* who committed murder – clearly Molly – meaning that he is Estella's father.

The final piece of the tragic puzzle now falls into place, and one of the novel's biggest mysteries is solved. Herbert has noticed a change in the convict, and his pitiful story also affects our view of him. ❂ Have your feelings for the convict changed since he first returned? Why?

We also learn the real source of his powerful attachment to Pip. When he met Pip in the churchyard, Herbert says, he *brought into his mind the little girl so tragically lost.* So, there has always been a connection between Pip and Estella – ironically, not the one that Pip assumed.

Chapter 51

◆ Pip visits Jaggers and confronts him with the fact that he knows Estella's mother (Molly) and father (Magwitch/Provis). Jaggers knows about Molly, but doesn't seem to know about Magwitch.

◆ Jaggers runs through a hypothetical case, pretending it's not a real one, more or less admitting that he tried to save Estella from a terrible life by giving her to Miss Havisham to adopt.

◆ He suggests to Pip that no purpose will be served by revealing the secret to anyone.

Pip feels he must confront Jaggers with the *bare truth.* ❂ Would you feel the same, in Pip's position? This is the only occasion in the novel when Jaggers – the focus of all the story's secrets – seems at all surprised. Besides Estella's background, he is also shocked to hear about Wemmick's home life and calls him a *cunning impostor.* Jaggers is also, we learn, much more sensitive to his surroundings than we might have thought. His feelings toward Estella – *here was one pretty little child out of the heap, who could be saved* – show a desire to do good that may surprise us.

For the moment, the secret is safe with the three characters, but it is obviously going to surface in the last few chapters of the novel.

Chapter 52

◆ Pip pays Clarriker to buy Herbert into his partnership. Herbert will be going abroad.
◆ It's now time to get Magwitch out of the country. As Pip's arm is injured, they decide to ask Startop to help row them to a steamboat, which will then take them to Hamburg.
◆ Pip receives an anonymous letter asking him to go to the limekiln on the marshes that night. He takes the coach there at once, not telling anyone.

The pace of the novel now accelerates rapidly. The plans for Magwitch's departure seem secure, but remember that although Compeyson has dropped out of the story, we know that he is in London and has possibly been following Pip.

The letter Pip receives gives the plot another twist. It also isolates him; no one knows where he is, and he is obviously in danger.

Over To you

? Add to your Mind Maps of Jaggers and Magwitch.
? Add any developments in Miss Havisham's character to your "women characters" diagram (p. 76).
? Locate new street names and settings on the London map (p. 30). Check the Kent map (p. 29) for the limekiln.

Chapter 53

◆ Pip meets Orlick at the limekiln at 9.00 P.M. Orlick is intending to kill Pip.
◆ Orlick ties Pip up and torments him. He was the one asleep on the stairs the night Magwitch came to Pip.
◆ Herbert, Startop, and Trabb's boy burst in and rescue Pip. They followed him to Kent after Herbert discovered Orlick's note.
◆ All the arrangements for getting Magwitch down the river are still in place and they are ready to go.

This episode in the novel shocks us with its almost supernatural horror. As the story gathers pace, the fear, tension, and violence focus, and finally erupt in this chapter and the next.

As Pip approaches the limekiln, he is overcome with foreboding, intensified by the atmosphere: *There was a melancholy wind, and the marshes were very dismal.* He doesn't expect to see Orlick. ✪ Did you expect him?

This scene is really very odd indeed and needs careful attention. Orlick has always been in the background of the novel, dangerous and brooding. Take a few minutes to go back over the Commentary, noting where Orlick appears. ✪ Do you think he is at all justified in hating Pip?

ORLICK'S REVENGE

Now take a close look at some of the things Orlick says in this terrifying scene: *"You was always in old Orlick's way since ever you was a child"*; *"It was you as did for your shrew sister . . . I tell you it was done through you . . . Now you pays for it."* This is the most extreme expression of the revenge theme we have come across so far, but it comes at a time when Pip is full of guilt and self-hatred. Dickens has drawn the scene to maximize Pip's suffering, while suggesting that nothing he has done has gone unnoticed or unpunished. He goes through the fire with Miss Havisham, but his suffering is not over; now Orlick presses the wound again, and fastens a rope around his neck. It's as close to hell as Pip gets in the novel. The moments before Orlick tries to kill him are filled with Pip's guilt, which goes beyond physical fear, as he imagines how everyone will despise him after his disappearance: *far more terrible than death was the dread of being misremembered after death.*

Orlick has been following Pip like a shadow, which is in a way exactly what he is—an evil reflection of everything that is destructive and cruel in Pip (a variation of the pursuit theme). Perhaps Pip hates him so much – *if I could have killed him, even in dying, I would have done it*, because he recognizes his own dark side in Orlick.

Whatever Dickens intended when he created Orlick, for us he is the strangest and most ambiguous character in the novel. This scene is the closest we ever get to understanding him.

Herbert and Startop's improbable pursuit of Pip to Kent reminds us that this is not a realistic novel, but a sensational story, where we often find ourselves believing things that are highly unlikely (who would have thought that Trabb's boy would come back?).

The last few paragraphs create a feeling of calm before the tension and further violence of Chapter 54. Dickens uses setting and atmosphere to prepare us: *the coming sun . . . I felt strong and well.* Compare with Chapter 20, another turning-point in the novel, when Pip is at the beginning of his moral and spiritual journey.

A quick recap

?   Jot down thoughts and ideas on Orlick in the form of a Mind Map.

now take a quick break before the grand finale

Chapter 54

◆ Herbert, Pip, and Startop pick up Magwitch at Mill Pond Bank and get him as far as Gravesend (Kent).

◆ Arriving at a riverside inn, they discover that a four-oared galley (a large rowing boat) has been seen going in the same direction.

◆ They continue their journey for many hours. As they approach the Hamburg steamer to board it, the galley pulls up alongside them. The river police on board demand that they give up Magwitch.

◆ Magwitch leans over into the galley and grabs hold of Compeyson. Both men fall into the river, struggling. Magwitch is badly injured, but Compeyson drowns, possibly killed by the paddles of the steamer.

◆ Magwitch goes to prison. Pip decides to stay with him as long as possible.

Pip is now behaving completely unselfishly, transformed from the social-climbing snob of the middle part of the novel. We are kept in a state of suspense; deep down, we know that Magwitch is not going to escape, but Pip's optimism makes us hope that he might – barely! Dickens uses atmosphere to convey this feeling of hope: *The crisp air, the sunlight, . . . the moving river itself . . . freshened me with new hope.* However, the convict's state of mind alerts us to the uncertainty of the future: *we can no more see to the bottom of the next few hours, than we can see to the bottom of this river.* Yet he is content to be with his *Faithful dear boy.*

As they move through Kent, Pip observes, *It was like my own marsh country, flat and monotonous,* and it's as if we're back to the beginning of the novel. The atmosphere changes, becoming more menacing: *There was the red sun . . . fast deepening into black* and this feeling of menace intensifies when they find out that they may have pursuers to contend with.

The scene where the police catch up with Magwitch is full of drama and tension and, like the previous chapter, focuses on the theme of revenge. Magwitch finally comes face to face with Compeyson and destroys him. The struggle begun so long ago finally ends in the water. Magwitch is a prisoner, again *manacled at the wrists and ankles,* and is severely injured. As a *returned*

Who are these two men?

transport (someone who has been transported abroad and who is breaking the law by returning), Magwitch will be punished by death.

Now all Pip's pride and selfishness have left him and he is prepared to stay with Magwitch until he dies. The paragraph, *For now . . . I had been to Joe* shows us how far he has grown in character and that he is now ready to do some good. He is at last able to love.

Pip's expectations have now evaporated. The final irony is that all Magwitch's property will be confiscated because of his criminal actions. So, his expectations, too, have come to nothing, although he never fully understands this.

Chapter 55

- ◆ Jaggers tells Pip that Magwitch will be condemned to death.
- ◆ Herbert goes to Cairo, leaving Clara behind with her dying father.
- ◆ Wemmick marries Miss Skiffins at a little church in Camberwell Green, with Pip as best man.

Pip is now becoming more and more isolated. Wemmick is married and Herbert, now engaged, is in Cairo.

The theme of loneliness now begins to dominate the novel, as Pip observes, *I had no home anywhere.*

Chapter 56

- ◆ Magwitch is very ill in the prison infirmary. Pip appeals for mercy, even writing to the Home Secretary. But Magwitch dies in prison with Pip beside him. As Magwitch is dying, Pip tells him that his daughter Estella is alive and well, and that Pip is in love with her.

It is impossible to remain unmoved by the intensity of emotion portrayed in this chapter. The convict is resigned and quiet, moving toward a peaceful death: *he would lie placidly . . . brightened it for an instant.* He feels that Pip has *seen some, small redeeming touch in him.*

○ Why do you think Pip reveals some of the truth about Estella to Magwitch, but not all? Do you think he does the right thing?

Chapter 57

◆ Pip becomes very ill with a fever. Joe comes to London and is there when Pip wakes up.

◆ Miss Havisham has died and has left £4000 to Matthew Pocket.

◆ Orlick is in jail.

◆ Joe cares for Pip. When he is better, Joe returns to the forge, having paid off Pip's debts.

◆ Pip decides to go back to Biddy and to ask her to marry him.

Pip is now quite alone, and his health finally breaks down. His delirium is vividly presented (Dickens himself had similar breakdowns on several occasions, and knew all about this kind of illness), and is almost like a death; when he wakes up and sees Joe, it's like being given a new life. Joe has forgiven him and his kindness moves Pip: *God bless this gentle Christian man!* His constant weeping suggests that all his pride has now gone and that his repentance is genuine.

Pip's journey is now almost complete; it has brought him back to Joe, and he is *like a child in his hands*. It is as if his life since leaving the forge has been a dream. The first time Joe takes him out is like being reborn: *Joe wrapped me up . . . of his great nature.* The world also seems new and fresh: *the rich summer . . . filled all the air.*

Dickens stresses that, compared to Pip, Joe had nothing to learn at the beginning of the novel. Pip has learned through his suffering, but Joe has remained the same, *just as simply faithful, and as simply right.*

Joe also shows great sensitivity and tact toward Pip by quietly paying off his debts and by slipping off quietly when Pip has recovered. In the end, Pip has to rely on Joe's money to get him out of trouble.

Chapter 58

◆ Pip returns to his hometown.
◆ Pumblechook interrupts his breakfast at the Blue Boar.
◆ Pip returns to Joe and Biddy to discover that it's their wedding day.
◆ Pip goes abroad to run the Eastern side of Clarriker's business. Years pass, and finally Clarriker tells Herbert about the help Pip has given him. They remain the best of friends.

The deception of Pumblechook and the cool response of the staff of the Blue Boar are final confirmation of the hollowness of Pip's success and the corrupting effect of his money.

Pip's hopes are still up as he approaches the forge and he is still planning his future. Even this last dream is shattered when he discovers, abruptly, that Joe and Biddy are married. This may rather surprise us, as there is a big age gap between these two characters, but it gives the plot great symmetry. Pip has to witness the successful pairing off of Wemmick and Miss Skiffins, Herbert and Clara, and now Joe and Biddy, while being shut out from happiness himself. ✪ Does Pip deserve Biddy, though? Does he deserve to be back at the forge?

Pip now becomes a wanderer, an exile from his own country. Dickens condenses the narrative, passing over many years and telling us that everything went well for Clarriker's business, although no one became very rich.

Chapter 59

◆ Pip returns to the forge and visits Joe and Biddy and their children.
◆ Satis House has been torn down. Pip wanders in the garden and bumps into Estella. Drummle is now dead.
◆ Dickens suggests that they will never part again.

This chapter was not in Dickens's original manuscript. His friend, Edward Bulwer Lytton, thought the actual ending was too sad and urged Dickens to unite Pip and Estella. Dickens was convinced by his arguments and made the change. He told his friend and biographer, John Forster, "I have put in as pretty a little piece of writing as I could."

In the published ending, Pip returns after eleven years to visit Biddy and Joe. Their son, little Pip, represents hope for the future and perhaps symbolizes Pip's change of heart.

When Pip visits the ruins of Satis House, we cannot help thinking of his false expectations and his ruined life. The atmosphere is quiet and melancholy, and there is nothing romantic about his reunion with Estella. Instead, Dickens describes their meeting with sadness and restraint. ✪ Is Pip right not to tell Estella about her father and mother?

The resemblance between Pip and Estella, which the convict observed, is strongest here. They have both been proud and then humbled; they both feel they have thrown away something valuable. Estella, like Pip, has *been bent and broken . . . into a better shape.* When we think of all these parallels, the possibility of their union is in keeping with the rest of the novel, though Dickens is right to leave it slightly ambiguous. He suggests a new beginning, *the evening mists were rising now,* but he only says that Pip *saw no shadow of another parting from her,* not that no parting ever occurred. Pip has never predicted events accurately, so as readers we are free to think what we want. Whatever we decide to believe about Pip and Estella, nothing can detract from the feeling of loss and sadness that hovers over the novel.

The ending

? Complete your convict Mind Map.

well done. You've finished the Commentary. Take a well-earned break

TOPICS FOR DISCUSSION AND BRAINSTORMING

One of the best ways to review is with one or more friends. If you're with someone who has studied the text, you'll find that the things you can't remember are different from the things your friend can't remember, so you'll be able to help each other.

Discussion will also help you to develop interesting new ideas that perhaps neither of you would have had alone. Use a brainstorming approach to tackle any of the topics listed below. Allow yourself to share whatever ideas come into your head, however silly they seem. This will get you thinking creatively.

Whether alone or with a friend, use Mind Mapping (see p. vi) to help you brainstorm and organize your ideas. If you are with a friend, use a large sheet of paper and colored pens.

Any of the topics below could appear on an exam, but even if you think you've found one in your exam, be sure to answer the precise question given.

TOPICS FOR DISCUSSION

1   Explain the changes in Pip during *Great Expectations*. How effectively does Dickens maintain the reader's interest in Pip's character?
2   Discuss Dickens's exploration of childhood.
3   Discuss the different ways in which Dickens examines the subject of love.
4   How significant is the role played by Jaggers?
5   Explain and discuss the importance of Joe Gargery.
6   Discuss and compare the roles of the women characters.
7   How important and significant are setting and atmosphere in the success of *Great Expectations*?
8   Explain and discuss the significance of the title *Great Expectations*.
9   Discuss the various examples of revenge in this novel.
10 Which of the coincidences in this novel seem most unbelievable?

In all your study, in coursework, and in exams, be aware of the following:

- **Characterization** – the characters and how we know about them (what they say and do, how the author describes them), their relationships, and how they develop.
- **Plot and structure** – what happens and how the plot is organized into parts or episodes.
- **Setting and atmosphere** – the changing scene and how it reflects the story (for example, a rugged landscape and storm reflecting a character's emotional difficulties).
- **Style and language** – the author's choice of words, and literary devices such as imagery, and how these reflect the mood.
- **Viewpoint** – how the story is told (for example, through an imaginary narrator, or in the third person but through the eyes of one character: "She was furious – how dare he!").
- **Social and historical context** – influences on the author (see Background in this guide).

Develop your ability to:

- Relate **detail** to **broader content, meaning, and style**.
- Show understanding of the author's **intentions, technique, and meaning** (brief and appropriate comparisons with other works by the same author will earn credits).
- Give **personal response and interpretation**, backed up by **examples** and short **quotations**.
- **Evaluate** the author's achievement (how far does the author succeed and why?).

Make sure you:

- Know how to use paragraphs correctly.
- Use a wide range of vocabulary and sentence structure.
- Use short appropriate quotations as **evidence** of your understanding of that part of the text.

THE EXAM ESSAY

Planning

A literary essay of about 250 to 400 words on a theme from *Great Expectations* will challenge your skills as an essay writer. It is worth taking some time to plan your essay carefully. An excellent way to do this is in the three stages below:

1 Make a **Mind Map** of your ideas on the theme suggested. Brainstorm and write down any ideas that pop into your head.
2 Taking ideas from your Mind Map, **organize** them into an outline choosing a logical sequence of information. Choose significant details and quotations to support your main thesis.
3 Be sure you have both a strong **opening paragraph** stating your main idea and giving the title and author of the literary work you will be discussing, and a **conclusion** that sums up your main points.

Writing and editing

Write your essay carefully, allowing at least five minutes at the end to check for errors of fact as well as for correct spelling, grammar, and punctuation.

REMEMBER!

Stick to the thesis you are trying to support and avoid unnecessary plot summary. Always support your ideas with relevant details and quotations from the text.

Model answer and plan

The next (and final) chapter consists of a model answer on a theme from *Great Expectations* followed by a Mind Map and an essay plan used to write it. Use these to get an idea of how an essay about *Great Expectations* might be organized and how to break up your information into a logical sequence of paragraphs.

Before reading the answer, you might like to do a plan of your own, then compare it with the example. The numbered points with comments at the end show why it's a good answer.

M ODEL ANSWER AND ESSAY PLAN

Explain the changes in Pip during the course of *Great Expectations*. How effectively does Dickens maintain the reader's interest in his character?

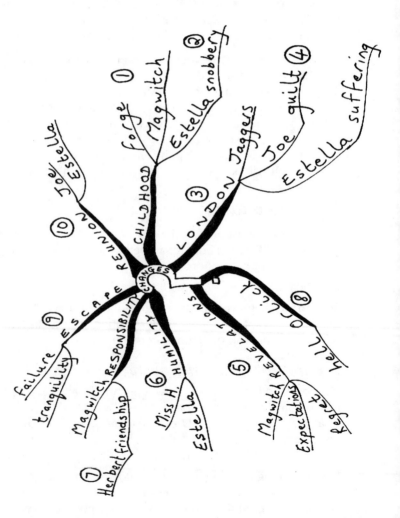

PLAN

1 Childhood. Encounter with convict.
2 Estella. Snobbery. Older Pip sees changes.
3 Rejection of Joe. Choice of crooked path.
4 Arrival in London. Corruption, disillusionment.
5 Central part of novel. Guilt, loss, suffering.
6 Revelation of benefactor. Collapse of expectations.
7 Return to Miss Havisham and Estella. Humility, awareness of mistakes.
8 Sense of responsibility for convict.
9 Suffering/hell. Orlick.
10 Tranquility with Magwitch.
11 Reunion with Joe.

ESSAY

Great Expectations follows Pip's progress through the pursuit of hollow ideals and incorrect moral choices, through suffering and disillusionment, to a final humility and wisdom. The wiser, "older Pip" tells his story in a cool, detached tone, shaping the narrative so that we are always aware of the bitterness of his loss of childhood innocence and of the heavy price he pays for his own mistakes. Telling the story in the first person insures that we are always in contact with the intensity of Pip's experiences and that he never really loses our sympathy.[1]

As a child, Pip's orphaned condition makes him completely dependent on his unpleasant sister and her saintly husband. Caught between Joe's kindness and her excesses, he grows up lonely, sensitive, and emotionally fragile. The convict brings fear and guilt into his isolated life, but Pip feels an instinctive sympathy for his outcast state: "I looked at the stars, and considered how awful it would be for a man to turn to face up to them as he froze to death, and see no help or pity in all the glittering multitude."[2] His encounter with the convict, which lays the foundation for all his moral growth in the novel, leaves him changed—more sober and more secretive.

The second formative encounter in the novel is with Miss Havisham and Estella. Of course, the two meetings are linked, as Magwitch is Estella's father, an irony that Dickens keeps hidden until near the end of the novel.[3] Estella awakens Pip's deep feelings of inadequacy and insecurity. She also triggers his descent into snobbery with her class-conscious criticisms: "I was much more ignorant than I had considered myself last night." He readily begins to pursue false values, a change that the older Pip acknowledges when he comments that the day "made great changes in me."

Pip's moving away from Joe and the wholesome values of the forge is motivated by greed. He rapidly descends into selfishness and is more than willing to grasp the opportunity offered by his great expectations without a second thought for Joe's feelings, admitting that he "was lost in the mazes of my future fortunes, and could not retrace the by-paths we had trodden together." The image of a journey on which he has lost the "true path" is resonant throughout the novel, guiding the reader to interpret his experiences correctly.[4] When he leaves Kent for London, he weeps again, perhaps conscious that he is leaving the best part of himself behind. The signpost marks a parting of the ways; Pip chooses the "crooked path."

London offers another maze of filthy and misleading byways. Pip finds it "rather ugly, crooked, narrow and dirty" – not the gold-paved streets of the fairy tales. He is under the control of Jaggers, whose obsession with power excludes any normal human feelings, for which Pip has to turn to his friends, Herbert and Wemmick. Both these characters have found their own ways of maintaining warm human values within a cruel and heartless society.

Pip's corruption is dramatically focused in the scene describing Joe's visit to London. The narrator is brutally frank: "I should have liked to run away," and shows a sharp awareness of his own shortcomings at the time: "I had neither the good sense nor the good feeling to know that this was all my fault, and that if I had been easier with Joe, Joe would have been easier with me."[5] As in the whole London section, we view Pip's development with mixed feelings of disgust, compassion, and frustration, aware all the time of how easy it would be to make the same mistakes.

The whole middle section of the novel centers on guilt over Joe: "I lived in a state of chronic uneasiness respecting my behavior to Joe," a general sense of loss (Pip describes himself as an unquiet spirit), and the intense suffering Estella causes him. The melancholy yearning of the narrative and the constant feeling of foreboding that permeates the story succeed in diminishing any criticisms we may have of Pip.[6] His constant awareness that there is "no fire like the forge fire" points toward his final return to the true (but static) values of the first part of the novel.

The most dramatic and, ultimately, the most productive of Pip's transformations takes place as a result of the convict's return and the collapse of his expectations at the end of the second stage of the novel. The revelation of his benefactor's identity brings Pip's hopes and dreams crashing down: "I began fully to know how wrecked I was, and how the ship in which I had sailed was gone to pieces." The shipwreck image widens the scope of Dickens's use of a physical journey to suggest symbolic meaning. The wreck is the beginning of Pip's regret and of his rebirth. Once he realizes the truth of his behavior toward Joe, "I could never, never, never, undo what I had done," he is ready to repent and to be forgiven.[7]

When he returns to Miss Havisham for the last time, he speaks with clarity and an awareness of his mistakes. He now wishes only to repay his debt to the convict and to make amends to Joe. The slow, painful growth of affection and a sense of responsibility for the convict draws warmth and closeness from the reader: "I little supposed my heart could ever be as heavy and anxious at parting from him as it was now." Pip's dependence on his friends – Herbert, Wemmick, Startop – also highlights the real value of human tenderness. At the same time, Pip's desire to help Herbert financially, and to persuade Miss Havisham to contribute, take a more prominent place in the narrative.[8]

This final process of growth also involves physical suffering—both in the fire at Satis House and at the limekiln, with Orlick, Pip seems to be undergoing a kind of purgatory, which will leave him physically reduced but spiritually renewed.

Ironically, in attempting to insure the convict's safety, Pip takes him peacefully to his death rather than to a hiding place, with all the concern and fidelity he showed as a child, but none of the fear. The full impact of the change is felt in Chapter 54, possibly the novel's most moving and tranquil chapter,[9] where Magwitch tells Pip what a pleasure it is to "sit here alonger my dear boy and have my smoke." Once he has completed his role with the convict, whom he recognizes as a "better person" than himself, Pip is ready to return to Joe.

His illness reduces him to a state of childlike dependency and enables Joe to resume his paternal role. Although Pip's future – whichever ending we accept – is likely to be an obscure and subdued one, the final image we have of him, completely humbled by the weight of his experiences, suggests a greatness of spirit that could only have been attained through mistakes, regret, and repentance: "Joe wrapped me up, took me in his arms . . . as if I were still the small helpless creature to whom he had so abundantly given of the wealth of his great nature."[10]

WHAT'S SO GOOD ABOUT IT?

1 Awareness of Pip's manipulation of narrative; "detached" – excellent use of vocabulary describing tone.
2 Pinpoints relationship between Pip and convict.
3 Shows good, clear essay structure.
4 Excellent observation of Dickens's use of metaphor.
5 This paragraph shows excellent use of quotation.
6 Clear focus on essay question.
7 Appropriate introduction of religious imagery here.
8 Effective movement of essay into the positive.
9 Evidence of enjoyment and personal engagement.
10 Personal response to endings and elegant return to essay title.

GLOSSARY OF LITERARY TERMS

alliteration   repetition of a sound at the beginnings of words, as in *ladies' lips.*

atmosphere   the general emotional tone of a passage, such as *gloomy*

context   the social and historical influences on the author.

foreshadowing   an indirect warning of things to come, often through imagery.

gothic   with a dramatic emphasis on death, decay, and mystery, as in some horror movies.

image   a kind of word picture used to make an idea come alive; for example, a **metaphor**, **simile**, or **personification** (see separate entries).

imagery   the kind of word picture used to make an idea come alive.

irony   **(1)** where the author or at least one character says the opposite of what they really think, or pretends ignorance of the true facts, usually for the sake of humor or ridicule; **(2)** where events turn out in what seems a particularly inappropriate way, as if mocking human effort.

metaphor   a description of a thing as if it were something essentially different but also in some way similar; for example, Wemmick's *square wooden face, whose expression seemed to have been imperfectly chipped out with a dull-edged chisel.*

narrative   storytelling.

personification   a description of something (such as fate) as if it were a person.

prose   language in which, unlike verse, there is no set number of syllables in a line, and no rhyming.

satirize   to criticize by ridicule, often ironic (see **irony (1)**, above).

setting   the place in which the action occurs, usually affecting the atmosphere; for example, the marshes.

simile   a comparison of two things that are different in most ways but similar in one important way; for example, *the wind rushing up the river shook the house that night, like discharges of a cannon, or breakings of a sea.*

structure   how the plot is organized.

theme   an idea explored by an author; for example, childhood

viewpoint   how the story is told; for example, through action, or in discussion between minor characters.